The Visitor's Guide
to
FRANCE: THE LOIRE

THE LOIRE

FRANCE

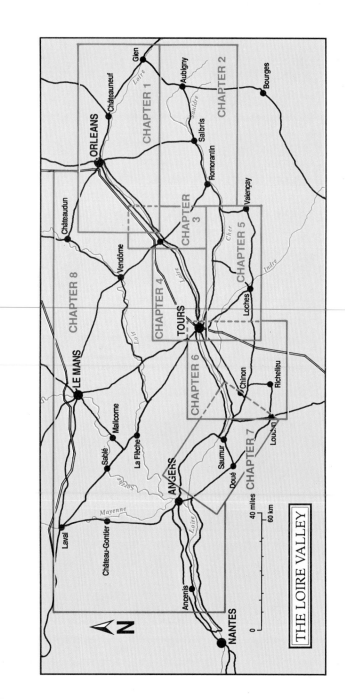

THE LOIRE VALLEY

THE
VISITOR'S GUIDE TO
FRANCE:
THE LOIRE

NORMAN BRANGHAM
&
MICHAEL DEAN

MPC

HUNTER
PUBLISHING INC

Published by:
Moorland Publishing Co Ltd,
Moor Farm Road,
Airfield Estate,
Ashbourne,
Derbyshire DE6 1HD
England

1st edition published 1985
    Reprinted 1986
2nd edition revised and enlarged
by Michael Dean 1990

ISBN 0 86190 371 4 (paperback)

Colour origination by:
Scantrans, Singapore

Printed in the UK by:
Richard Clay Ltd, Bungay, Suffolk

Published in the USA by:
Hunter Publishing Inc,
300 Raritan Center Parkway,
CN 94, Edison, NJ 08818
ISBN 1 55650 265 6 (USA)

British Library Cataloguing in
Publication Data:
Brangham, A.N. (Arthur Norman),
1916-86
    The visitor's guide to France. -
    2nd ed. - (Visitor's guides.
    Loire
    1. France. Loire Valley - Visitor's
    guides
    I. Title II. Dean, Michael *1936-*
    III. Brangham, A.N.
    (Arthur Norman), *1916-86* .
    Visitor's guide to the Loire, 1985
    IV. Series
    914.4504839

Cover photograph:
Château Chambord
(International Photobank).

Illustrations have been supplied as
follows: H. Alcock: pp 43 (both), 46
(both), 50, 51, 55 (both), 58 (both),
59, 66 (top), 67 (top), 87, 90
(bottom), 91 (top), 98 (bottom), 107
(both), 119, 122, 123, 126, 127; M.
Dean: pp 14-15, 23, 35, 63, 66
(bottom), 75, 83, 86, 91 (bottom),
103, 106 (both), 111; French
Government Tourist Office: pp 11,
31, 74, 114 (bottom), 115;
Photostore: pp 67 (bottom), 98
(top), 99 (top), 114 (top); H. Race: p
82; SNCF: p 10; P. Tavener: pp 130,
131, 134-5; Touraine Regional
Tourist Board: pp 79, 90 (top), 102;
P.J. Wilson: p 99 (bottom).

CONTENTS

Key to Symbols Used in Text Margin and on Maps

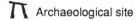 Archaeological site

 Church/Ecclesiastical site

Nature reserve/Animal interest

 Building of interest

 Garden

 Castle/Fortification

Sports facilities

 Museum/Art gallery

Cave

 Beautiful view/Scenery, Natural phenomenon

Watersports

Other place of interest

Key to Maps

▬▬▬	Main road		Town/City
═══	Motorway		Lake
River			Forest/Parks

INTRODUCTION

Guide books often find the ancient or medieval divisions of a modern country mark the most recognisable and convenient boundaries around which to base their information. France is no different; Brittany, Burgundy and Provence are all good examples of this. So habitual is it to refer to areas of France by their pre-Revolution, provincial names that they seem to constitute natural, self-contained entities.

The Loire Valley does not fall into this category. Its name is better known than many French provinces, whether contemporary or medieval. At various times, small provinces and counties — Maine, Anjou, Touraine, Blois, Orléans and Berry — have sat astride what is conventionally understood as the Loire Valley. Anjou and Touraine are the only names still in common use; they take up the lion's share of the Valley.

The French Revolution, with its fiery nationalism and hatred of all things *ancien*, did away with the old provinces, their regional councils and partial autonomy. The new regime introduced the *départements*. These remain today almost exactly as they did 200 years ago.

Designed so that the government's chief officer — the *préfet* — could reach any part of his area within a single day on horseback, the *départements* were given names that could not be linked with the Ancien Régime. In the Loire Valley, natural features, especially the rivers, provided the new names. Thus came Sarthe, Maine-et-Loire, Loir-et-Cher, Mayenne, and so on.

The *département* remains the core, the backbone of the French system of government. Even so, contemporary society and needs have led to the grouping of *départements* into economic regions. Consequently, the visitor may come across Centre (which is centred

7

on Orléans), and Pays de la Loire (which is centred on Nantes). Most of Pays de la Loire has nothing whatsoever to do with the Loire or the Loire Valley.

The Loire Valley is, of course, châteaux country. Châteaux and the colourful lives of their inhabitants make this part of France world-famous. However, it is ironic that the area with the most châteaux — the Loire Valley — does not cover the whole length of the Loire. In fact, very few of the châteaux are actually on the river. It is generally accepted that the Loire Valley is the middle section of the river, starting between Gien and Châteauneuf-sur-Loire and ending somewhere around Angers. In essence, this covers the area from where the river turns from its northerly progress to south-westerly, to just before where the sea's influence begins to dominate the river.

So this book takes as its limits the upstream point of Gien, and the downstream one of Ancenis; with a wide band stretching north and south, as the key Loire tributaries cast their influence. This covers the main features and the famous châteaux, as well as the characters and events that are central to the role the Loire Valley has played in France's history.

The Loire is the longest river in France, stretching about 1,012km (628 miles). It rises out of a high plateau in Vivarais (Ardèche) just below the rounded hump of Mont Gerbier-de-Jonc. Its rivulet life begins at 1,400m (4,600ft) and sets off briskly in a southerly direction through pasturelands. It is diverted north-west at Rieutord by the massive Mont Suc de Bauzon, but for whose presence the Loire would have made its way to the Mediterranean. Instead, it passes through the cold and sparsely inhabited uplands of Auvergne to the dramatic volcanic site of Le Puy-en-Velay.

The river then works its way through a series of gorges, complete with the occasional dam, to Roanne. It is below Roanne that the river begins to slow and open out, leaving the highlands behind. This arrival at the lower ground also marks the start of the Loire's traditional alliance with transport. The Canal de Roanne à Digoin begins here, running parallel to the river; it is the first in a series that follow the river right down to Briare, just above Gien. The Loire itself now continues onwards, along the edge of Burgundy, passing comfortable riverside towns such as Digoin, Decize, and Nevers (tracked all the way by the canal).

Just below Nevers, the major tributary of the Allier joins the Loire, to be followed now by a steady succession of other rivers, large and small. From the south they flow down from the Massif Central; from the north they flow out of the Armorican Massif. Below Nevers the river also touches its first wine names — Sancerre and Pouilly. At Briare, the canal, which has followed the river since Roanne, crosses the Loire by means of a superb aqueduct, designed and built by Gustav Eiffel. The canal continues northwards to join the Seine and, ultimately, to pass Eiffel's greater claim to fame in Paris. The canal does this because the Loire begins its long sweep westwards between Briare and Gien. Orléans lies at the most northern point of this great arc.

This change of direction occurs because the river is deflected by the harder rocks to the north. Various geological changes in the Tertiary Era, when the Alpine folding occurred and the Massif Central was being formed, combined with a westward tilting of the land and the River Loire changed its direction. Otherwise the Loire would have simply been an important tributary of the Seine. As it was, the Atlantic Ocean was able to flow inland as far as the area around Tours (hence the shell marls on either side of the river). The Loire itself, coming up against the sea, deposited much clay material in the area below Orléans, thereby creating the Sologne.

As the sea retreated, so the Loire followed it westward, creating a richly fertile, alluvial plain, commonly known as the 'Garden of France'. Beyond Tours and Angers, the river heads for the sea. Below Nantes it becomes a wide estuary, bordered by the famous dockyards, and crossed only by the modern toll-bridge. Eventually, the River Loire loses itself in the Atlantic off the Vendée and Brittany coasts. Surprisingly for one of the longest rivers in Europe, the Loire has remained relatively unspoilt. Unlike the other major rivers, such as the Rhine or the Danube, there is no commercial traffic afloat, and very little industry is visible on the banks. As a result, the valley retains considerable charm and character.

In this great flood-plain there are almost no naturally dramatic features such as mountain folds, ravines or striking rocky outcrops. It is flat in the Sologne; elsewhere there are gentle undulations whose high points do not reach 200m (650ft) until you come to the rising ground east of the Aubigny-sur-Nère to Bourges road where some hills touch 300m (980ft). In a landscape of horizontal planes, the eye is drawn to the vertical lines of chalk cliffs set back from river banks.

A view from the top of these modest escarpments provides a fresh perspective. At one's feet are the carpetlands of glinting rivers and an expanding horizon. From this gentle elevation it is possible to pick out each individual poplar tree along the river's edge. Beyond, the trees are compressed into dense, foreshortened woodlands that hide the open parklands, meadows, heaths and farm-plots. A balanced,

TGV high-speed trains can travel from Paris to Tours in less than an hour

well-tempered panorama is laid out underneath a large sky.

The châteaux are the architectural expression of this landscape. The Renaissance had an important bearing on the Loire Valley and still imbues its character, contours and peoples.

The people, here in the true centre of France, are like their landscape. They judge themselves reasonable, good-natured and well-balanced. They live in a comfortable, indulgent land where sanity and moderation prevail. The people of Anjou are known for their good-naturedness; the *douceur Angevine.* In Touraine they claim to speak the purest French, and children are sent here to learn the language.

The people of the whole region are sometimes referred to as Vallerots. The people of Anjou are Angevins; those of Touraine, Tourangeaux; of Blois, Blésois; of Orléans, Orléannais. The name Ligerians for the inhabitants of the valley is appropriate, because the Roman name for the Loire was *Liger.*

Climate

Like its people and landscape, the area's climate is moderate. One season tends to merge into the next in gentle transition. It compares with southern England's, except that the mid-summer months along the Loire tend to be warmer. For the visitor, it means a season which can stretch from April to November.

Spring comes early; the first wild flowers show at the end of February. A variety of early vegetables thrive in the temperate climate and fertile alluvial soil. A moist, warm wind prevails from the Atlantic, so that the average rainfall diminishes further inland. Frosts can recur into April and short, sharp storms are not unknown in May and June. Summer is the period of high pressure systems over the Azores but the Atlantic breezes moderate excessive temperatures.

Typically, summer skies of Anjou and Touraine are wide, pale blue and dotted with cotton-wool balls of clouds — signs of fine weather. Delicate pastel colours of riverside buildings and trees reflect in the lazy waters of the rivers. The Loire itself looks delectably placid; slow, shallow waters slip past yellow, sandy islets sprouting osiers. Clear yellow patches of sunlight filter through the light

A more relaxed form of transport in the Valley

greens of poplars and willows. Note how the river banks have been built up with massive embankments (*levées*), constructed and repaired over the centuries to hold in the floods which used to devastate low-lying lands. In addition, they now keep the riverside roads open.

In winter, the serene river swells with the turbulent rush of water as rain and snow in the uplands drain into the Loire's huge catchment area which covers the whole of central France. Sand bars and islets are swept away; new ones emerge. Vast quantities of debris are carried down to make the Loire shallow and unnavigable.

Plant and Animal Life

In the gardens of the Loire Valley, climbing roses, day lilies and morning glories consistently flower some weeks earlier than they do in Britain, a sign that here the temperatures are, on average, a shade warmer.

Along roadside verges one may suddenly come upon great carpets of light green and yellow euphorbias. The scattered sentinels of tall asphodels stand on parade for hundreds of metres, their white flowers almost done and their stems turning to straw in early summer. To see commonplace plants and trees in a fresh setting gives them a fresh lustre: here is a thumb-nail impression of blossom time in late spring.

Ecological pressures resulting from industrialisation and the intensification of farming have not been as great in the Valley as elsewhere. A greater variety of indigenous species flourish. As an example, corn-cockles, corn-marigolds, cornflowers and orchids have been found in the vicinity of Troo on the Loir.

In areas of intensive monoculture, diversity of wildlife has been reduced. This is noticeable, for instance, where large fields have been given over to oil-seed rape crops.

River banks which have escaped too much human interference provide delightful glimpses and sounds of birdlife ranging from ducks to kingfishers. Hoopoes emit their hollow 'hoo-poo-poo' notes in the woodlands; the golden oriole alternates between a flute-like call and a raucous, cat-like cry. From the thickets come the liquid call and musical song of the nightingales.

The great diversity of birdlife is in the lowland plateau of the Sologne. Its damp heaths and deciduous woodland contain many shallow, reed-fringed pools; the haunt of purple and night herons, bitterns, ducks, harriers, stilts, godwits, gulls, terns and warblers. Some of these birds can also be watched in the Forêt d'Orléans beyond the north bank of the Loire. In Sologne, take care not to trespass when birdwatching; it is possible to be taken for a poacher.

In Sologne and wherever there are deciduous woods and small lakes there are red and roe deer, wild boar, hares, pheasant and partridge. Beech martens, pine voles, edible dormice and red squirrels have all been recorded in such habitats.

Otters can often be seen, especially on the islets along the quieter reaches of the River Vienne. In the muddy waters of ponds, ditches and gently flowing backwaters, the European pond tortoise is sometimes seen. Again, in moist places at night, you will hear the pure piping notes of the midwife toad.

For the entomologist, the spring air is filled with the penetrating song of crickets in uncultivated fields. Equally loud but rougher, are the bursts of stridulation from great, green bush-crickets on an afternoon or night in late summer.

About forty species of butterfly occur in the region. Fritillaries, graylings, blues and skippers can be seen during their flight periods of first or second broods. The lepidopterist may even come across the scarce swallowtail (*le flambé* to the French) flying in early or late summer.

The Historical Background

Although the Loire Valley is, of course, best known for its châteaux, it has played a central role in the history of France since the very earliest times.

Primitive stone implements have been unearthed in many places. They testify to the presence of small human communities along the banks of the Loire and its tributaries between 400,000 and 150,000 years ago during the Lower Palaeolithic. Museum drawers supply the evidence of flint tools, small differences among the working of these are significant to specialist prehistorians. However, lay curiosity is also aroused. To begin with, there is the question of how these unknown people eked out a living. Then there was the problem of adapting during cycles of great climatic changes when the vegetation and the creatures it supported also altered radically. Adaptation seems to have been skilful. Stone tools were modified to allow effective hunting of new species of game which the changed environment nurtured.

Periodically, other small groups of people migrated into the region and brought with them original ideas, so that alien and indigenous cultures fused. For the most part, as long as the environment remained the same there was little incentive to improve on

Sunflower fields are a common sight in the Loire

existing tools and techniques. The Loire Valley could not emulate the magnificent cave art of Périgord further south. This was because the soft chalk provided neither the durable surface nor the constancy of temperature and humidity which the limestone caves and rock-shelters supplied to their Upper Palaeolithic contemporaries.

The last Ice Age moved away northwards some 10,000 years ago. Dense forests covered much of the region. Men hunted, gathered berries and fished in the wider, shallower and more placid waters of the rivers. Deer antlers were fashioned into harpoons. As the climate grew warmer, the big mammals left, and new tools, suited to trapping smaller mammals such as rabbits, had to be invented.

The Loire has always been the highway by which cultural innovations and destructions have been introduced, moving downstream in the direction of the Atlantic. In the fourth millennium an invasion

which had its origins in the Danube Basin introduced stock-raising. It was a product of the so-called 'Neolithic Revolution' which had begun in the eastern Mediterranean. Europe's economic and social structures were transformed by this revolution. The Loire peoples resisted it for a while for the good reason that theirs was chiefly a forest industry unsuited to a pastoral system. However, a cooler, drier climate superseded the previous moist, warm Atlantic phase, and forest clearings were more easily created. Stock-raising established itself, though on a relatively small scale. Wheat and barley were introduced in the Early Neolithic but agriculture was confined to the plateaux where wind-born loess — fine, fertile dust — reduced the density of the woodlands. This prepared the way for the rich granary-lands of the Beauce today.

The Danubian settlers built large rectangular wooden houses, erected the first funerary monuments — passage graves or *dolmens à couloir* — and developed distinctive types of pottery.

About 2,500BC — the Middle Neolithic — dolmens of the Loire developed a characteristic Angevin form by which a simple portico replaced the traditional passage, and the monument became more elongated. Some very large dolmens can be seen; the one at Bagneux outside Saumur is one of the largest in France and those outside Gennes are a similar size. By taking the D571 east from Angers in the direction of Saumur, you will be able to find a number of dolmens and menhirs. Alternatively, north of Tours, is the impressive dolmen outside Mettray, hidden by a copse, called Grotte aux Fées.

Less spectacular Neolithic remains can be searched out. They are the *polissoirs*, boulders on which stone axes were regularly sharpened. Usually found near streams, these hard buff-stones betray their one-time function by the smooth parallel grooves, striations which have survived for 5,000 years.

In the late Neolithic — the period between 2,500 and 1,700BC — at Le Grand Pressigny (a little south of the Valley) there was a 'factory' which exploited easily worked and high quality flint. It turned out large daggers, new types of arrowhead which were leaf-and lozenge-shaped and tanged, exporting these articles all over Europe. The Musée de la Préhistoire in the château at Le Grand Pressigny is an important one and gives a very good idea of the Stone Age implements produced in the vicinity.

As long as tools were only made of stone, there were great limitations imposed on development. However, local communities did extend their farming activities to less fertile soils, and the exploitation of the land began to take on a pattern which was to persist for many centuries. Their dwellings must have been built of very light materials, for no traces of them have been found, nor did they leave any grave-goods.

Gold and copper ornaments and copper daggers appeared, as well as high quality beaker-ware. The source of this culture's diffusion is still a matter of conjecture. The people who brought the Beaker Culture seemed to infiltrate into populations of the late Neolithic and had no territories of their own. The Chalcolithic (copper) culture was superseded by bronze. The Bronze Age lasted some 1,200 years until about 600BC. It was an important development for the Loire Valley where metal-working centres were set up. Bronze is an alloy of copper with a high percentage of tin, and the latter was mined extensively in the lower reaches of the Loire. A vigorous export trade in flanged axes and palstaves flourished. During that time collective megalithic graves gave way to individual cremation in urns which were placed in cemeteries by the Urnfield peoples who spread westwards along the Loire and its tributaries between 1,100 and 800BC. Fertility figures which had been widely worshipped by Neolithic peoples lost out to more abstract symbolism.

Long-distance trade routes were established, for copper and bronze came originally from the eastern Mediterranean. Bronze Age Phoenicians sailed up the Loire to trade. Hoards of copper ingots have been found near Bourges and Azay-le-Rideau. Metalwork was taught in the Valley, and craftsmen spread far and wide from there. Metalware was also imported from England and Ireland. Axes, swords and bronze ornaments were constantly evolving until the arrival of the Iron Age, between 800 and 600 BC, made many of these artefacts obsolete. The Iron Age produced superb craftsmen and trade expanded still further.

With the approach of the written record of history, a general picture emerges of a thriving Loire Valley civilisation, its industries and outlooks modified by both peaceful and violent invasions from the innovative east. Among the most influential of these invaders were the Central European Celts. Between 1,200 and 800BC, the Celts, called Carnutes, founded Chartres, Orléans, Blois and Amboise, using the Rivers Loire and Cher for commercial traffic. Mining, metallurgy and farming prospered. It was evidently a lively society but politically backward, as was to be demonstrated in their confrontations with the Romans.

As the Roman conquest of Gaul moved northwards, Caesar's soldiers found themselves facing Celts who belonged to an aristocracy which enjoyed luxury and military heroics. Their shields and weapons were magnificently decorated; their warlike rituals were Homeric and blood-curdling. They were headstrong, valiant, hardworking, quarrelsome and inconsistent. They revered their Druids and their poets. Each chieftain was surrounded by a faithful band of personal followers. Peasants, herdsmen and artisans who were not part of the élite lived in scattered villages and farms.

The Loire Valley belonged to that large area of Gaul, between the Rhine, the Cevennes and the Atlantic coast, which was known as *Gallia Comata* ('Long-haired Gaul').

Caesar resolved to conquer the whole of Gaul in 58BC and the tribes of the Loire submitted without much resistance. The tribes were the Namnetes on the north side of the Loire estuary and inland beyond Nantes; the Pictones occupied the other side of the river. The Turones (around Tours) straddled the middle Loire and the Cher, making Tours their main river-port built on pile foundations. North of them were the Andecavi.

The Carnutes held the land between what is now Paris and Orléans (*Genabum*), building a riverside port here, as well as at Amboise and Blois. The Celtic name for Blois was *Bleiz* or *Blaiz*, which was 'wolf' in Celtic, an indication of the inhospitable, wolf-infested forestlands of the Blésois. To the south, the Biturges had *Avaricum* (Bourges) as their capital.

By 52BC unrest had spread among the tribes. They swooped on *Genabum*, 'led by two desperadoes', writes Caesar in *The Conquest of Gaul*, killing the Roman traders who lived in the town. Caesar came from Italy to quell the uprising. *Genabum*, which guarded a bridge across the river, was quickly captured and the booty distributed among the Roman troops. Then Caesar marched into Sologne to make the difficult attack on *Avaricum* (Bourges), perhaps camping, as some historians think, at Romorantin, as part of his struggle against his main enemy, Vercingetorix.

In the course of his campaigns in the Loire Valley, Caesar had boats built at Nazelles (*Navicellis*), a village behind Amboise, in preparation for his attack on Tours (*Turonum*). During the final rebellion in 52-51BC, Caesar again had to fight in the vicinity of the Loire during a particularly cold winter. He turned this to his advantage by billetting his soldiers in the relative comfort of his headquarters at *Genabum*, while the Celts suffered the elements out in the open. There were further skirmishes and further victories for Caesar. Having satisfied himself that Gaul was pacified, he laid down generous conditions of subjection. 'By these means it was easy to induce a people exhausted by so many defeats to live in peace', he concludes in *The Conquest of Gaul*.

Roman occupation brought many material benefits; agriculture was improved, the vine was introduced and roads were built. The main highway was that from *Lutetia* (Paris), the capital of the Parisii tribe, through *Genabum*, along the north bank of the *Liger* to *Caesarodunum* (Tours). From here, one road led south to *Limonum* (Limoges) and Aquitaine, another continued along the north side of the Loire to its mouth. Some of today's arrow-straight roads follow the Roman foundations.

Tax collecting was left to local magistrates. Under Emperor Augustus, the Loire became the boundary between the northern province of *Lugdunensis* and the southern one of *Aquitania*; it remained the political division for 300 years. Prosperous towns were concentrated on the river which was used for the transport of goods. Major towns, like Orléans, commanded bridges over the river. During 300 years of Roman domination, the region prospered and stayed at peace.

In place of the one-time Gaulish kings, who were already being discarded before the Roman conquest, magistrates or *vergobrets* were elected. However, powerful chiefs still ruled over their broad lands and commanded private armies.

As was customary under Roman rule, local religion was respected as long as it did not contravene Roman law. Gaulish Druids — wise men drawn from the ruling classes who maintained Celtic traditions and myths and held powers of life and death — had to be removed; they were seen as a potential source of political unrest. The Druid's annual meeting point had been at Fleury, a suburb of St Benoît-sur-Loire, their consecrated ground at the 'umbilical centre' of Gaul.

Of the handsome Roman towns and their public buildings which were essential to Roman garrisons — baths, aqueducts and amphitheatres — not much remains by comparison with Provence. However, there are more fragments than might be imagined.

A few examples will serve. In the basilica of St Benoît, the chancel floor is a Roman mosaic brought from Italy. In Orléans, the base of the Tour Blanche is Gallo-Roman. A section of the city wall and a round tower of Tours, built about AD275, have been exposed. A little to the west of Thésée (*Thascica*), on the Cher, is a Roman ruin called *Mansio de Manselles*. It had been a *mansio*, or staging-post, of Roman troops on the road between Bourges and Tours. *Thascica* was marked on the famous Peutinger map of the third century, and such *mansiones* were sited roughly every 40km (25 miles).

A Roman *cippus*, a cylindrical pagan altar, with carved warriors round it, is in the Church of St Ours in Loches, doing duty as a font. North-east of Luynes are thirty-five columns and several arches of the Roman aqueduct which supplied Tours with water. Eight kilometres (5 miles) west, at Cinq Mars-la-Pile, stands a massive square tower on the top of a cliff; its function is still a subject of speculation. At St Maur, the abbey, founded in the sixth century, stands on the site of a Roman fountain whose basin is beneath the chapel; lead pipes and some of the bases of the Roman arches are visible. Nearby, at Gennes, fragments of an aqueduct and *nymphaeum*, as well as the foundations of an amphitheatre have been revealed, all suggesting that Gennes had been an important station in Roman times.

Archaeologists have excavated the sites of Gallo-Roman houses in the Sologne. One at Millançay in the Forêt de Bruadan (a name of Celtic origin), and another at Montrieux-en-Sologne, suggest that the basis of Solognot agriculture was cattle in open pastures, rye and vines in the clearings.

Some authorities think that an evangelist, Altin, came to this part of central Gaul to convert the inhabitants to Christianity as early as the first century. He is said to have arrived with Savinius, one of the seventy-two disciples sent by the apostle Peter. Similarly, St Maurice came to Angers. St Gatien went to Tours a little later as the first, but clandestine, Bishop of Tours. When Constantine the Great was emperor in the fourth century his conversion to Christianity made it the official religion of the Roman Empire.

St Martin was the most famous of all evangelists in the Loire Valley. He, like all the other evangelists of those times, had been a soldier with the Roman legions. All were 'foreigners'; St Martin was Hungarian. This arose because the Romans recruited men from Greece and Hungary to protect the frontiers of Gaul from invasion by Germanic tribes. St Martin was still wearing Roman uniform when he cut his cape in half to give one part of it to a beggar. Living a frugal life in the chalk caves of Marmoutier, he was elected Bishop of Tours and founded the Abbey of Marmoutier in 372. So great was his popularity with the people of Tours that when he died the city became a major focus of pilgrimage. A whole town, *Martinopolis*, had to be built a little to the west of Gallo-Roman Tours to accommodate the influx. A visit to the cave cells of St Martin, St Gatien, St Denis, St Brice and St Patrick is part of the tour of Marmoutier Abbey.

Once the Roman defences of Gaul had given way, the Loire Valley, after centuries of stability, fell prey to invasions. Asian and German hordes came from the east; first Attila the Hun, then Childeric and the Franks. The Franks crossed the Rhine and, under their young king Clovis (he came to the throne in 481 at the age of 15), captured much of north-west France. Orléans became his capital. Later, this daring and ruthless man became a Christian, partly to please his determined wife, partly to gain the support of the Church. During his conquest, he halted his armies on the north bank of the Loire at Amboise. On the opposite bank lay the territory of the Visigoths under Alaric who had acquired the once Roman province of Aquitaine. In 503 the two kings met, choosing as neutral ground the Ile d'Or (now a campsite) in the middle of the river. They swore eternal friendship. Milestones on mounds of earth, known as *donges*, marked the boundary, and one such mound is still visible at Sublaines, south of Amboise. Four years later, Clovis fell on the Visigoths at Vouillée, killed Alaric with his own hands, and drove the enemy almost to the Pyrénées.

Clovis died in 511. His kingdom of the Franks was not unlike the territory of France today. He had thrown back the Huns from the gates of Orléans in 451 under the inspired leadership of the Bishop of St Aignan. Clovis had run his kingdom like a private estate, so when he died that estate was parcelled out among his sons. This dynasty of Merovingian kings became weaker and the dynasty ended in 752, but not before the Arab advance from Spain had been crushed. In 751 they had reached the plateau north of Poitiers. Their defeat by Charles Martel ('the Hammer') finally destroyed Musulman aspirations in northern France.

Under Charlemagne (742-814) literature and learning flourished. Priories and churches were built. Alcuin of York lived and taught at the Abbey of Cormery which was founded in 791. Alcuin, perhaps the most distinguished scholar of his day, taught the Emperor's family and members of the court. He came to Cormery in 796, and continued to spread his civilising influence until his death there in 804. A similar influence was wielded by Bishop Théodulfe who founded the first university at Orléans and gave free lectures.

Charlemagne reigned for 46 years, and the Loire region was but a tiny fragment of his great empire; Normandy and Brittany were not part of it. Fragments of the Carolingian presence are the mosaic in the Church of Germigny-des-Prés; another was found beneath Orléans Cathedral. A ninth-century church is in the crypt of St Solenne in Blois. There are others in Tours, St Benoît-sur-Loire, Bourgueil, Cravant and Chinon.

Abbeys and priories were a cultural counterflow to the chaos which constant wars and quarrels between local warlords threatened. Not only were they centres of religious observance, they also served as places of refuge. They were seats of learning where ancient texts were preserved, studied and copied, as well as shelters and hospitals for travellers and pilgrims. They often tried out new methods of agriculture in their gardens. Marmoutier was one of the most prestigious abbeys in Christendom; Cormery's prominence can be attributed to Alcuin. The Benedictine Abbey of St Benoît-sur-Loire had been founded in 650 and was at its peak under Charlemagne and Charles the Bald in the ninth century. Orléans, too, was an important centre. Finally, there was the Chartreuse du Liget, founded by Henry II of England in reparation for the assassination of Thomas à Becket at Canterbury.

When the Frankish Empire of Charlemagne collapsed, East Franks became Germans; West Franks became French. The frontier between them was never clearly defined, so there are those who have argued that this oversight sowed the seeds of 1,000 years of hostility between France and Germany.

Charlemagne's successors lacked his charismatic power to hold his racially disparate empire together. Through the laws of inheritance, the empire was divided into three kingdoms. What we know as France, excluding Brittany, became the Kingdom of Charles. The king was too weak to defend his peoples and repel the Viking-Norman invaders who landed at the mouth of the Loire and ravaged all the lands between Nantes and Orléans. The first king of the Capetian dynasty, Hugues Capet (938-96), hardly dared move out of his capital of Orléans. Real power lay with his feudal vassals such as the Counts of Anjou, Touraine, Blois and Maine. They did as they chose: raised armies, built castles, appointed bishops and minted their own money. War between one county and another was incessant. Fortresses were erected everywhere as a consequence of these disputes.

Supreme among the fortress builders was Count Foulques III, known as Foulques Nerra, The Black Falcon (971-1040). He was a skilful general who built innumerable square keeps, mainly due to the feuds with his neighbour, the Count of Blois. First, he put up temporary constructions of wood, a stockade on top of an earthwork, known as a *plessis*. This name recurs in these parts, although all signs of the original forts have disappeared. Permanent stone fortresses replaced the *plessis* at strategic points. Those at Loches, Montbazon and Montrichard are among the remnants of Foulques Nerra's handiwork.

In those early, cheerless, cramped stone keeps, everyone ate and slept on the first floor. By the thirteenth century, fortresses were becoming more spacious with separate kitchens and bedrooms, a change introduced by Crusaders returning from Palestine. As more refined instruments of war were devised, square towers gave way to round ones to reduce the efficacy of grappling-hooks. Walls were reinforced to thwart the sappers. Angers' massive castle sums up medieval ideas on defence. Not until the sixteenth century did gracious palaces begin to supplant the castles, where moats and dungeons were more decorative than useful. A century later, châteaux were designed for social ostentation and amusement, surrounded by ornamental gardens.

The name of Foulques Nerra begins the tangled history of Anjou and the kings of England. Anjou had come into existence in the seventh or eighth century; Foulques I was the founder of a bellicose Angevin family. A later Foulques fought Henry I of England, and his son Geoffrey married Henry's daughter Matilda in 1129. Out of this union came Henry Plantagenet, born at Le Mans in 1133 (the name derives from the habit of the first Counts of Anjou of wearing a sprig

Typical Loire countryside

of *genista* — broom — in their hats).

By the age of 18, Henry had inherited Normandy, Anjou and Touraine (ceded to France in 1242). When Louis VII of France divorced his young and vivacious wife Eleanor in 1152, Henry Plantagenet thought that marriage to her would aid his interests. Before it happened, a touch of romantic farce crept in. Henry's younger brother, who was only 16, took a fancy to Eleanor, 12 years his senior, and tried to kidnap her. Then the son of the Count of Champagne attempted the same at Tours. Eleanor evaded them both, married Henry, her former husband's arch rival, and brought Aquitaine as her dowry. Henry ruled from the English Channel to the Pyrénées. On the death of King Stephen in 1154 (himself a Count of Blois), Henry acquired the throne of England as grandson of Henry I and great-grandson of William the Conqueror. It was by such quirks of fate that he became Henry II of England and eight Plantagenet kings ruled until the death of Richard II in 1399.

Henry II spent half his life in France. Eleanor set up her own court in Poitiers. She urged her sons John Lackland and Richard Coeur-de-Lion (the Lionheart) to side with the French king against their father. Henry II died at Chinon in 1189 during the struggles with his sons. He, Queen Eleanor and Richard I all have their tombs at Fontevraud Abbey. When John Lackland succeeded his brother Richard as king of England, he lost Anjou to King Philippe-Auguste of France, only for it to be recaptured under Henry V and Henry VI. In 1444, Anjou returned nominally to France, though the king's direct rule of the duchy did not take place until 1584.

Last of the Angevin dukes was 'Good King René' under whose rule the duchy flowered. His court was at Angers and, for a short while, it became a major European town. His kingship was the titular one of Sicily; his other fiefdom was Provence, and he died at Aix-en-Provence in 1480. His wide learning, gentle manner and genuine concern for his people's welfare made him much loved but unsuited to the political intrigue and military decisiveness which his responsibilities demanded. He avoided the castles of Angers and Saumur, preferring to stay in the small manor houses which he had built or bought close to the forests where he could hunt.

One of the last counts of Blois was so debt-ridden that he sold his country to the Count of Orléans and, in 1498, Blois was incorporated into the kingdom of France.

From the tenth to the sixteenth centuries, Orléans was either the capital of the French 'royal demesne' when it was virtually confined to the Ile de France, or second capital to Paris until the last of the Orléans-Angoulême dynasty in Henri III.

Technically, the English monarch in his French territories was a vassal of the King of France; in practice, he was often the more powerful. Constant territorial disputes between them and repeated English invasions of France helped foment the Hundred Years' War (1338-1453). Attacks and counter-attacks were punctuated by truces and realignment of allies. It was a brutal and desolating war. In 1422 the English entered Paris; Orléans was invested; the English, with their Burgundian allies, controlled all northern France except Brittany.

French morale was low, leadership from the Dauphin, as Charles VII was called until his coronation, was lacking. He was a pathetic, haunted creature; weak and vacillating, ill-fed, dressed in wretched clothes and without money, he scuttled from one château in the Loire to another.

In 1429, Joan of Arc came on the scene. She lived only 19 years (1412-1431). Driven by her 'voices' she confronted the Dauphin at Chinon. She was allowed to join the forces mustering for the relief of Orléans. Without any position of command, she placed herself at the head of the army in full armour. Orléans was relieved and this defeat of the English was the turning point in the war. The English were pushed out of the Loire Valley with the recapture of Beaugency and Jargeau, and defeated at Patay. The impetuous Joan then led the Dauphin through hostile country for him to be crowned at Reims. During an ill-advised attack on Paris, Joan was wounded. Then the king's money ran out and he disbanded his army for the winter. In 1430, she was captured by the Burgundians at Compiègne, sold to the English who had her tried for sorcery by the Inquisition, and found guilty. She died at the stake in Rouen; Charles VII did not raise a finger in her defence.

The Maid was canonised in 1920. The impetus she had created continued to give the French heart for further attacks on the English. The latter lost Normandy and Bordeaux; the Burgundians became less enthusiastic allies; all that was left to the crown of England was Calais. Thus, The Hundred Year's War dragged to its dishonourable conclusion.

After Joan of Arc had been put to death, Charles VII, no longer merely 'King of Bourges', as he had been sarcastically called, but King of France, developed into a powerful monarch. He created a strong, well-paid army which put down his nobles' private wars; he effectively reorganised the tax system. For this, he enlisted the help of an immensely wealthy merchant of Bourges, Jacques Coeur (1395-1456). He restored the prosperity of France almost single-handedly. In Bourges, his monument is his superb *hôtel*, the pigeon loft in its attic roof can still be seen; pigeons were his means of keeping in touch with his agents all over Europe.

Jacques Coeur, as Controller of the Mint, court banker and controller of the king's finances, wielded vast power. However, in 1451 he was falsely charged with complicity in poisoning the king's lovely mistress, Agnès Sorel, who had been installed in the Château of Loches. Coeur left France to die on the island of Chios. He was not a nobleman and he represented a new class of successful merchants — the bourgeoisie — a class which was to stamp its character on the Loire Valley.

It is worth considering here — as the Loire Valley enters its great period of châteaux building — just what a château actually is. A dictionary definition, while correct, covers everything from a castle to a stately home. This is very much the problem when looking at châteaux, especially in the Loire Valley. The Valley encompasses the whole range of styles of building of châteaux, and it is possible to see how each stage slowly replaced the preceding one.

Initially châteaux were no more than castles, fortresses, or fortified manor houses. As time went on, and the power of the French Crown created a form of political stability, so the design of the château changed — especially as Italian Renaissance influence spread — and the stately home and country house style gradually evolved. This took about 400 years, between the fourteenth and seventeenth centuries, although the great period for the Loire Valley lasted only 150 years. However, the great attraction of the Loire Valley is that this whole period of development in architectural styles and design is summarised in such a small area. Significantly, much of the building, especially towards the end of the period, was undertaken by the new class, the bourgeoisie.

These rich merchants and financiers bought up land throughout the Loire Valley, especially Touraine, and asserted their influence on monarch, court, and the Valley. King Louis XI (1423-83) lived in the grim fortress of Plessis-lès-Tours, surrounded by these successful new businessmen.

Louis' Controller of the Treasury was Jean Bourré who built himself the Château of Plessis-Bourré which combined medieval defences on the lower floors with comfort, light, air and space provided by large windows above. The château had to receive the king and his court from time to time and provide entertainment. Tours, Langeais, Chenonceau, Azay-le-Rideau, Villandry and Le Clos-Lucé are all examples of châteaux built by the powerful financiers of the fifteenth and sixteenth centuries. They also bought town mansions and renovated them to standards of appropriate magnificence.

Rulers held court in their various royal châteaux: Angers, Blois, Plessis-lès Tours, Amboise, Loches, Chambord and Chinon. To be near the king, the merchants positioned their châteaux along the Loire, the centre of political, financial and religious decisions. Here were concentrated the shrewdest and most ambitious figures who salvaged the nation's economy and stimulated diverse industrial enterprises. Louis XI himself introduced mulberry trees, silkworms and silk-making to the region.

The Development of the Château

Tenth-Twelfth Century
Angers, Chinon, Loches
Simple, fortified keeps, designed for defence; arrow slits; no windows.
(British equivalents: Tower of London, Windsor)

Thirteenth-Fourteenth Century
Langeais, Saumur, Sully
Transition from Gothic to Renaissance; thick walls; separate rooms; windows; corner towers with positions for attacking besiegers.
(British equivalents: Bodiam, Penhurst)

Fifteenth Century
Blois, Chaumont, Plessis-Bourré, Gien
The use of gunpowder and cannon brought the realisation that the castle was no longer militarily tenable. Complex defence systems of towers; conical roofs; some comfort.
(British equivalents: Hever, Herstmonceaux)

Sixteenth Century
Amboise, Azay, Chambord, Blois, Chenonceau, Villandry
Renaissance influence at its height. Large windows; sculpture and pattern brickwork; extravagant furnishings. Sites on, or near, water.
(British equivalents: Hampton Court, St James)

Seventeenth Century
Beauregard, Blois, Cheverny
Military aspect disappears in favour of stately home. Gardens and water, growth of Classical influence. Court moves back to Paris.
(British equivalents: Audley End, Hatfield House)

Eighteenth Century
Montgeoffroy, Ménars
Châteaux building declines and is replaced by creation of vistas.
(British equivalents: Buckingham Palace, Blenheim)

Towards the end of the fifteenth century the Italian Renaissance found its way into the Valley. Charles VIII (1470-98) had invaded Lombardy. When he was forced to retreat he brought back with him Italian artists and art treasures as loot. Everything Italian became fashionable. The architectural assimilation was slow but harmonious, as can be seen at Chambord, Azay-le-Rideau and mansions such as Hôtel Pincé in Angers and Hôtel d'Alluye in Blois. High Renaissance was the apogee of flaunted luxury. The stimulus to ostentation was the intense rivalry between courtiers.

The Italians introduced major innovations in architecture, sculpture, medal-making, embroidery, gardening and gastronomy. Two of the most famous Italian artists were Francesco Laurana and Girolamo della Robbia. The latter's well-known terracotta medallions, which he produced at Orléans, were much in demand.

Leonardo da Vinci (1452-1519), the universal genius, was brought to Amboise by François I (1494-1547). He worked at Le Clos-Lucé for the last 3 years of his life. Among his imaginative projects were plans for a canal between Tours and Lyon and he had schemes to improve the Loire region. Many of his plans can be seen in the museum at Le Clos-Lucé. Amboise's reputation was immensely heightened by Leonardo's presence there.

The most significant political influence was Catherine de Medici (1519-89). By her marriage to Henri II she exerted much authority as queen, while after his death in 1559, she was a queen-regent with absolute power. She was almost the embodiment of the Italian Renaissance in France. Her well-intentioned policy of equal support for Catholics and Protestants contained the seeds of its own destruction. Caught in a web of intrigue in her particularly odious family, she was disliked by most ordinary French people, and sneered at as a tradesman's daughter by French nobility.

Great native talent arose at the same time. The lyric poet Pierre de Ronsard (1524-85), born near Vendôme, and François Rabelais (1495-1553), physician and satirist, a native of Chinon, added further lustre.

Below the appearance of opulence there was latent conflict. Catherine de Medici had been unable to resolve the growing intolerance and bitterness between the rapidly enlarging faction of Protestant Huguenot dissidents and Catholics supporting a weak monarch. The Wars of Religion broke out in 1562. Murder and abductions were commonplace. Blois, Orléans and Amboise (where Catherine de Medici and Mary Stuart witnessed the slaughter of Protestant plotters) were the scenes of massacres and reprisals. Churches and abbeys were sacked by the Huguenots. Henri IV's Edict of Tolerance, prepared at Angers and signed in Nantes in 1598, brought peace but it was revoked 87 years later.

With the death of Catherine de Medici the vitality ebbed from the Loire Valley. The royal châteaux were used less and less. The court moved to Versailles under Louis XIV, the 'Sun King'.

Industries suffered a decline only to revive and expand, for the river remained the cheapest form of transport. Sugar refineries were started between Nantes and Orléans. The Rivers Loire and Seine were linked by the construction of the Briare Canal. Distilleries were set up, canvas factories were established at Angers, and Saumur made cotton goods. Printed fabrics were in such demand that Nantes, Angers and Orléans were all turning them out. In addition, Orléans had factories making stockings and vinegar. Later, in 1790, the first steam-driven cotton-spinning machinery was installed in all three towns.

The Duc de Penthièvre, grandson of Louis XIV, instituted a silk factory at Châteauneuf-sur-Loire as part of his benevolent scheme to provide work in the district. The manufacture of steel at Amboise was established by the Duc de Choiseul.

Theoretically, the Loire Valley ought to have been the scene of particularly intense bitterness as France careered towards the Revolution of 1789. Despotic government, corruption, maladministration, unfair tax burdens, favouritism towards the clergy, class privilege and greed brought about unrest. In the Valley, absentee landlords visited their châteaux for pleasure and ostentation, neglecting their estates and the workers on them. However, the violence in the Valley was less than might have been expected. The margins rather than the heart of the region experienced the main upheavals. As far as the Revolution is concerned, it can also be said that there was less poverty than elsewhere. Vineyards flourished; the soil encouraged intensive cultivation, even though there were huge expanses — the Sologne in particular — which were dismally unproductive.

In the wake of the Revolution itself, many factories closed and industries declined. Some vindictive and haphazard desecration of châteaux by Republican extremists — the *sans-culottes* — took place. The properties of Catholic Royalists were sequestered. Angers embraced the heady notions of revolution with enthusiasm. Its cathedral was sacked and renamed a 'Temple of Reason'.

Following the outrage at the execution of Louis XVI in 1793, at the persecution of the clergy, and at mass *levées* for the Republican army, an insurrection flared at St Florent-sur-Loire. It spread to Angers and south into Vendée, and the Vendée War was conducted by Catholic Royalists (the 'Whites') against the Convention (the 'Blues').

After the defeat of the Royalists in 1794, the Republicans shot or guillotined thousands in Angers. Not until 1801 was reconciliation achieved, through the indefatigable work of the Angevin, Abbé Bernier who was made Bishop of Orléans by Napoleon. The Valley settled down to a compromise administration within its new *départements*. Republicans dominated the towns, Catholics and Royalists controlled the country where they rebuilt the châteaux and retained the *métairie* system. This meant that peasants farmed the land and shared the profit with the landlord, bred cattle, and ensured the livings of the rural priests.

Despite the lesser revolutions of 1830 and 1848, general prosperity continued through the development of rural industries. Napoleon III ordered drainage and replanting in the once fever-ridden Sologne. The same man blundered into war with Prussia in 1870. The French were defeated at Sedan, the Emperor surrendered and Paris was invested. Tours was made a capital from which the national defence was conducted by Gambetta, who had escaped from Paris by balloon. The Germans advanced as far as the Loire where a French force awaited them at Orléans and was driven back. On the road to Blois, the tiny 'Army of the Loire' repulsed the Germans only to be defeated soon afterwards. Tours was bombarded and then occupied.

In World War I the Loire played its traditional role as an outpost of Paris, to fall back on in times of retreat. Tours was a base for United States troops.

During World War II the treasures of the Louvre were stored in the Château of Chambord. Tours became the temporary seat of the French government. Here the question of an armistice was seriously raised for the first time. Orléans and Tours were heavily damaged by bombardment; by the Germans in 1940 and later by Allied air forces. In 1940, French military resistance was crushed in a few weeks and for a time all was chaos. At Saumur, the tiny, ill-equipped force of the Military School, ignoring orders to retreat, held three Loire bridges for more than 24 hours before running out of ammunition and able-bodied cadets.

On 24 October 1940, Montoire on the Loir was chosen as the meeting-place between Adolf Hitler and the aged Marshal Pétain, Head of State of what was to be known as the Vichy Government. They met in a railway carriage in the station, near a railway tunnel, in case the RAF should attack the town. The River Loire became the boundary between occupied France to the north and unoccupied France to the south.

In the post-war period, Tours and Orléans have been extensively reconstructed, and both towns have expanded enormously. Traditional rural activities continue to flourish: vines, fruits, vegetables, mushrooms, flowers and all the delicacies of the table. The new crop of oil-seed rape's brilliant yellow flowers can be seen from afar. Well-established industries stand side-by-side with newer ones: printing,

A characteristic small hotel in the Loire

pharmaceuticals, glass-works, perfumeries, metallurgy, shoe-making and nuclear energy plants. Orléans university is large and American in style. The government aims at decentralisation — a bone of contention of many years' standing. Orléans, so easily reached from Paris, represents the first logical place for such a policy to be applied and, as a result, the Valley has kept in step with the general post-war prosperity of France.

It is ironic, however, that today's prosperity is achieved without the River Loire being able to fulfil its age-old role as a trading highway. Now it is purely the decorative artery of the region, unused except for occasional pleasure boats. Gone are the powerful guilds which ensured the rights of their members to make a living transporting goods along the river. Gone too are the tolls, levies and various designs of boats able to navigate the idiosyncracies of current and shoal. The chief vessel in the past was the *chaland*; flat-bottomed, without a keel, steered by a massive oar and pole. The Musée de la Marine de la Loire at Châteauneuf-sur-Loire reconstructs the history of river life.

Accommodation

The residents of the Loire Valley have had plenty of experience of welcoming visitors to their part of the world. Today's visitor is offered an excellent range of accommodation, suiting most people and most price budgets.

Hotels are classified under the French national statutory system using stars, from one star (simple, basic) to four stars (luxury). Not surprisingly, the cost usually increases with the greater number of stars a hotel has. However, the number of stars does not guarantee the quality of service a visitor receives. As a result, it is possible to have a perfectly acceptable stay in a one star hotel, and a disappointing stay in a four star hotel. Whatever type or grade of hotel is used, the visitor pays for the room rather than per person. Almost without exception, prices in all but the very top quality hotels represent excellent value for money. Breakfast usually carries an extra charge, and it is the custom to take dinner in the hotel restaurant (where the hotel has one) especially if it is a family-run establishment.

It is possible to tour the Loire Valley without making onward reservations at almost any time of the year. Where this is done, though, the visitor is well-advised to begin looking for a hotel for the night from around 4pm. There are plenty of hotel guides to help with the selection although some local tourist offices offer a reservation service (and are often the best option). Despite its idiosyncracies, an up-to-date red Michelin guide to France is an invaluable aid; although others swear by Gault-Millau or other guides. It is also worth obtaining a copy of the annual guide of the Logis et Auberges de France from the French National Tourist Office. This contains information on about 5,000 small hotels and inns situated in less important towns and villages. These inns are fairly simple and straightforward, perfectly comfortable and excellent value for money, quite often working out at the equivalent of less than £10 per head per night. The simple furnishings are often more than compensated for by the standard of the meals.

For those seeking a little bit more, there are a number of hotel groups offering either a corporate, or a consistent, style of accommodation. Ibis and Campanile are the names the visitor is most likely to come across. Both offer good, two star accommodation at reasonable cost, with restaurant facilities; they are frequently on the edge of town. Both chains can offer onward reservations, if required, at no cost. At the three star level, Novotel (who also own Ibis) are fairly widespread, and are very comfortable. Children who share their parents room are usually excluded from the price.

At the top end of the scale, the Loire Valley has its fair share of top quality hotels. For those seeking something a little special, and very much in character with the area, the Relais et Châteaux consortium offers accommodation in châteaux and country houses. These are generally privately owned, and the visitor is treated almost as a guest of the family. They are not cheap but will provide some superb memories.

A word of caution: French hotels are awarded stars for their comfort. Visualise a one- or two-star hotel, for instance, to be comfortable in the sense of being equipped with cosy, relaxing public rooms, and you may be disappointed. Lounges, bars and television rooms tend to be uncomfortable and stark. Rather than place the emphasis on comfort before food, the French have taken the opposite viewpoint.

When you book a room, a deposit (*verser des arrhes*) may be asked for. This understandable precaution on the part of hoteliers is caused by the fact that an increasing percentage of travellers do not turn up to honour their booking. Reserve a room for the same evening and the hotelier may request an arrival not later than 6 o'clock, after which time the room will be let to the first caller. It is advisable to allow for unexpected delays in driving to the hotel, especially during the high season.

Half-board arrangements with the hotel satisfy most people. This allows the whole day to be spent sightseeing. Stay three nights or more and favourable half-pension terms may well be available. Some hotels, especially in larger towns, provide only bed and breakfast; this is convenient for trying out different restaurants each day. Ideally, however, eat in the hotel's restaurant unless its cuisine is not up to standard. This will allow the visitor to get to know the character and atmosphere better, and to judge the variety of its menus.

For the more independently minded, *chambres d'hôte* — the French equivalent of bed and breakfast — are widely available. One usually stays in a house, again almost as a guest, but *chambres d'hôte* are often in rural situations. Evening meals are sometimes available — it is worth checking. This is an excellent way to capture the true character of the Valley.

The serious Francophile who intends to spend a bit of time in the

Loire Valley is best advised to find a base from which to tour. The best way to do this is to rent a *gîte*. *Gîtes* are cottages which are usually in a rural location. They are all checked by the local tourist board and let out to visitors. However, it is necessary to book in advance. You cater for yourself but that is very much part of the experience — buying food from the local shops or the market, or quite often from the farm on which the *gîte* is located. The whole idea is also flexible enough that eating out is possible, as is a long day touring with a late return.

Gîtes are graded under a system which uses the symbol of ears of corn (*épis*), from the simple (1 *épi*) to the comfortable (3 *épis*). An historical or particularly comfortable *gîte* can also be graded *de caractère* (with character). *Gîtes* can be booked in France through the regional tourist boards or through several tour operators.

Campers and caravanners will find plenty of good campsites right through the Valley, again ranging from the simple to the luxurious. Most towns have their own *camping municipal,* although standards do vary. The green Michelin guide to camping and caravanning (*Guide Michelin Camping et Caravaning*)is a useful aid. For those who do not want to load all their camping gear, a number of tour operators offer holidays and short-stays in pre-erected tents complete with all the necessary equipment. Camping in the countryside — *camping sauvage* — is generally frowned upon. It is certainly advisable to obtain a landowner's permission.

Youth hostels are available throughout the region but you need to be a member of a national youth hostelling association to be able to use the facilities. For those with a bit more time to spare, there are many other holiday opportunities which allow the exploration of all or part of the Loire Valley. Boating, horse-drawn caravans, and walking are just some ideas — see the Tips for Travellers section for more details. The regional tourist offices also have information on other options.

The Local Cuisine

Wherever one goes and wherever one stays in the Loire Valley, the food is straightforward, filling and of good quality. The 'Garden of France' has plenty of ingredients from which to choose and the local people have a long established reputation for hearty eating. It is no surprise that Francois Rabelais' great creation, Gargantua, hailed from this part of France.

Today, Rabelaisian and Gargantuan *bons viveurs* are no more common in Touraine than anywhere else. In any event, the distinc-

Markets selling freshly grown produce are popular

tion of the regional cuisine lies in its simplicity. It is a curious fact that no outstandingly great regional dishes have sprung from the Loire Valley although, historically, it was the birthplace of French cuisine. Just as the Loire Valley absorbed, then modified the sixteenth-century Italian Renaissance architecture introduced by Catherine de Medici as Queen-regent of France, so it at first copied, then subtly altered the work of Catherine's Italian chefs. While the monarchs of France either ruled from their royal châteaux along the Loire, or returned to them for relaxation from Versailles, gastronomic standards were maintained. Sophisticated Paris is so near by way of autoroutes, and food-conscious visitors descend annually on the valley. They help to sustain those high standards, as the ratings in Michelin and other gastronomic guides confirm.

A benevolent climate and soil ensure the abundance of vegetables, fruits and vines; forests provide the game; rivers and meres the fish. The ingredients for a restaurant meal of quality are always to hand. The least expensive *menu touristique* is likely to offer simple, standard dishes (though cheapness is not necessarily a bar to quality ingredients and careful cooking). If food interests you, be prepared to pay more, and look out for regional specialities. These include shad (*alose*), either stuffed (*farcie*) or with sorrel sauce (*à l'oseille*), and pike (*brochet*) served with a creamy butter sauce with wine vinegar and shallots (*beurre blanc*). Pike is a ubiquitous fish, and may appear as delicate *quenelles de brochet* (a light, sausage-shaped soufflé) or as young pike served like whitebait.

Loire salmon (*saumon*) is considered to be among the finest in France, though there is less of it now; *saumon à la Chambord*, cooked in red wine, is a sought-after delicacy. Eels (*anguilles*) often feature on menus. They may be stewed in wine on their own or with other fish to make a *matellote*, or fried whole in breadcrumbs with other small river fish to make *friture de la Loire*. Another alternative is to have them minced, baked and served cold as *terrine d'anguille*.

Pork, the chief local meat, is served traditionally with prunes (*noisettes de porc aux pruneaux*). Sologne, south of Orléans, is the main source of game: hare (*lièvre*), Sologne jugged hare (*civet de lièvre de Sologne*), rabbit (*lapin*) or young rabbit (*lapereau*). You may also be served boar (*sanglier*) in autumn and winter. Many varieties of pâte are produced. Of the many vegetables grown locally, asparagus (*asperges*), broad beans (*fèves*) and cardoons (*cardons*) are especially good.

Specialities associated with towns are numerous but they are not always easy to come by. Look out for *Andouillettes*, chitterling sausages from Angers and Jargeau, as well as *andouilles* (cold smoked sausages) and *boudin de volaille à la Richelieu*, a sausage made of truffles, mushrooms and chicken. *Cernaux au verjus* is a Touraine *hors d'oeuvres* of green walnuts in grape juice, salt, pepper and chervil; *chouée*, a dish of cabbage and butter is an Angevin delicacy. Other specialities include *jambon de volaille*, chicken legs stuffed with ham from Richelieu; *quiche Tourangelle*, an open tart of minced potted pork, the latter being the delicately flavoured *rillettes de Tours;* and *rillauds*, cooked pieces of breast of pork, served hot at Angers. There is also *beuchelle à la Tourangelle*, mushrooms and cream with kidneys and sweetbreads as well as *truffiat*, potato cake. Orléans' contribution is its mustard and wine vinegar.

Apples, pears (William pears are used in an *eau-de-vie*), peaches, plums of Tours, strawberries of Orléans, melons of Langeais, quinces, cherries (especially from Olivet), dessert grapes, and an apricot-peach known as *alberge de Tours*, are some of the local fruits. Various sweet dishes are made with them. Apples stuffed with jam and baked are *bourdaines*. In Anjou, cherries are called *guignes*, and a *guignolet* liqueur is made from them. Angers is the home of Cointreau where many fruit liqueurs are produced. A pear in syrup with liqueur and ice-cream is known as *poire belle angevine*. Slices of caramelised apples or pears covered in pastry make *tarte des Demoiselles Tatin*. A popular jelly is made of quinces and is called *cotignac* (those of Orléans are said to be outstanding), and a quince cheese is also made (*pâté de cotignac*), to say nothing of an *eau-de-vie des coings*.

Cheese boards and specialist shops display an interesting variety of cheeses. Goats' cheeses are more widespread than cows'. Of the former, the most common are *Ste Maure*; these are soft, cylindrical and sometimes called *chèvre long*. Similar to *Ste Maure* are *Villebarou* and *Ligueil*, all these are at their best between May and November. *Romorantin* (or *Selles-sur-Cher*) is dark, blue-skinned and nutty. Similar cheeses come from Troo and Montoire. *Valençay* (or *pyramide* because of its shape) is firm, medium strong and nutty; so is *Levroux*. *Crémets* are small, fresh goat cheeses; they are eaten with sugar and cream and are a speciality of Anjou.

The chief cow's milk cheese is *Olivet-bleu*, factory-made and inn-oculated with mould. It is small and circular, sometimes wrapped in leaves, and best between October and June. *Olivet-cendré* looks similar, and is ripened in charcoal ash — its best eating period being between November and July. Closely related are *Vendôme bleu* or *cendré* (best between October and June), *frinault affiné*, *Villiers* and *St Benoît* (the latter's surface is rubbed with salt and charcoal).

As a result of the close connection between the kings of England and their lands in Anjou and Touraine, Loire wines have for long been familiar to the English nobility and merchants. They liked their Loire wines white, sweet and strong. They were known as Andega-vie wines which had been transported first to Nantes and then carried by sea to English ports.

Loire wines are becoming increasingly popular. They are light, crisp, pleasant and, for the most part, relatively inexpensive. Some experts say that the Loire *vins de table* are superior in quality to their counterparts from elsewhere in France.

Expensive wines are not necessarily the most enjoyable comple-ment to a meal. Local ones can be appropriate even though they do not have an *Appellation Contrôlée* (AC or AOC) which guarantees the authenticity of the bottle's contents. Some of the cheaper wines, both *Vin Délimité de Qualité Superieure* (VDQS) — regarded as inferior to AC wines — and the modest *Vin de Pays* which specifies the *dépar-tement* or area it comes from, are often very good indeed.

The first wine-producing area properly within the region is the Coteaux d'Ancenis, making a light, dry rosé. From around Angers come other rosés; the dry Rosé du Loire and the slightly sweet Rosé d'Anjou. Also on the north bank of the river are dry white wines with a rich 'nose', the Savennières (Coulée-de-Serrant and Roche-aux-Moines) which, because of the smallness of the vineyards, command very high prices. South of Angers, the Coteaux du Layon are sweet white wines which go well with quail or ham.

Saumur is the next district; its vineyards spread south beyond Montreuil-Bellay. Some red wine is produced, though Anjou is not generally associated with red wines. Saumur whites are the abundant crops, maturing in the natural chalk caves which are cool enough to make warm clothing necessary, even on a hot summer's day. Saumur sparkling wine bears more than a passing resemblance to champagne, for the grapes are grown on similar soil, but they are decidedly cheaper than champagne. Anjou pétillant, a faintly sparkling rosé, is also made.

Entering Touraine, and surrounding the towns of Chinon and Bourgueil, are vineyards which produce two famous wines. North of the river, the dark red, fruity Bourgueil carries a scent of raspberries. Chinon wine, from both sides of the River Vienne, was Rabelais' local drink, and that is said to smell of violets. Bourgueil and Chinon are not easy to tell apart. Both are supple and fragrant; perhaps Bourgueil is a little more robust, and Chinon softer. You are supposed to drink Chinon out of a special glass, a round bowl curving outwards towards the top. Such glasses can be bought in Chinon shops. They have Rabelais' head and shoulders etched on the glass, along with a quotation from the great man: *'Beuvez tousjours, Ne mourrais jamais'* (Keep drinking, you'll never die). Try drinking both Bourgueil and Chinon chilled with *hors d'oeuvre*, and *chambré* with a main course of white meat.

Moving north of Tours to the River Loir, the visitor comes to the Coteaux du Loir, which produces mostly dry white wines. Clos de Jasnières, with a tiny and sought-after output, is fruitier and slightly sweeter than most wines of the Loir Valley, and resembles Vouvray. In the vicinity of La Chartre-sur-le-Loir are the wines of La Chartre, Marçon, Ruillé and Vouvray-sur-Loir. Further east again are the Coteaux du Vendômois wines; these include Jasnières, which is a quality wine.

Return to the larger vineyards of the Loire. The Sauvignon de Touraine is dry, flowery and inexpensive; the best of these is the aromatic Azay-le-Rideau. Touraine Gamay is a red wine made from the same grape as Beaujolais, and their flavours are similar. The wine museum in Tours deals with social history of the regional wine-vine.

East of Tours is Vouvray whose *route du vin* starts at Noizay, 8km (5 miles) further east. Vouvray's sparkling *vin mousseux* is, like those of Anjou, Touraine and Montlouis, an *Appellation Contrôlée*. One dry (*brut*) Touraine is called *vin vif* instead of *mousseux*. Grapes in the Vouvray area are harvested late — towards the end of October — for the bunches to become infected with the 'noble rot' fungus, *la pourriture noble*. This makes the skin shrivel and the grape dry out to produce the sweet yet sharp, still wine, whose quality varies from year to year. On the opposite side of the river to Vouvray, the Montlouis vineyards produce a sparkling wine which is saddled with the doubtful label of 'poor man's Vouvray'.

At Amboise, some reds and a dry rosé are made. Thereafter come the less distinguished Vins de l'Orléannais and Coteaux du Gennois. However, in the seventeenth century the English held the wines of Orléans in high esteem. They were red and yellowish wines which were spoken of as 'clarets' and reckoned to be among the best in France.

Away from the Loire itself are small and interesting vineyards which have to be searched out, for they are true local wines which are mainly sold only in the district. Quincy and Reuilly, west of Bourges; Valençay and Cheverny (the latter appears on some hotel wine-lists); Menetou-Salon (rather like Sancerre), are examples. Just beyond Loire Valley boundaries are the famous vineyards of Sancerre and Pouilly-sur-Loire where the delectable Pouilly-fumé comes from.

The region offers a stimulating array of wines, varied in character and flavour, deriving from the small variations and blends of soil — clay, chalk, alluvium, sand and pebbles — of the river valleys. Here the *vins du pays*, drunk perhaps as a carafe wine, can be surprisingly agreeable.

The Loire Valley has a whole wealth of history and culture waiting to be discovered and explored. Whether the visitor stays just a couple of days, or a couple of weeks, the region offers something new around every corner of its attractive roads and lanes.

1
FROM GIEN TO BLOIS BY THE LOIRE

Gien, the traditional upstream end of the Loire Valley, is a very pleasant small town on the banks of the river. Extensively damaged during World War II, it has re-established itself as an ideal starting point for an exploration down the Loire. The town has one of the oldest château sites in the Loire Valley, although the present building dates from the fifteenth century. The château houses the Musée International de la Chasse — a museum of hunting which provides a fascinating insight into many of the traditions of the local area. The château buildings have been well-restored in their own right and there is a good view of the river from the terraces.

Gien was the first town on the Loire that Joan of Arc reached on her journey to find the Dauphin at Chinon. She is commemorated in the name of the town's church, although she certainly would not recognise any of its contemporary architecture. Gien is best-known for its earthenware pottery. The factory, which still turns out expensive handmade items in the traditional fashion, is situated on the western edge of the town, on the quayside. Visits to the factory can be arranged but these do need to be booked in advance.

Quaysides and raised embankments, called *levées*, run alongside the Loire for almost its whole length. They were originally built to try to control the flow and the potential destructiveness of winter floods. This was an attempt to help the river trade but, ironically, they contributed to its decline. The roads along the top of the *levées* were as quick, if not quicker, than the boats themselves.

A short diversion upstream from Gien to Briare of 10km (6 miles) allows a visit to Eiffel's superb aqueduct that carries the Canal

Latéral à la Loire over the river. North-east of Gien and north of Briare is the Château de la Bussière, which contains an interesting fishing museum. From Gien it is possible to work your way through the Sologne to Blois — this route is followed in the next chapter. To follow the Loire itself, it is possible to use either the D952, which skirts the edge of Orléans Forest or, alternatively, cross the bridge at Gien and follow the D951 to Sully. Those on foot can follow one of the national long-distance footpaths called Grandes Randonnées. The GR3 follows the Loire right the way downstream, often passing through the wooded areas, but certainly visiting most of the places of interest. As a different route, GR3c runs across the Sologne, joining up with GR3 again near Chambord.

The D951 runs to Sully-sur-Loire, and passes opposite the Dam- pierre nuclear power station (one of many on the Loire). Those interested in visiting the station itself need to follow the D952 from Gien, and follow the signs. There is an observation point but advance booking is needed for the guided tour. Dampierre village itself is a pleasant halt or, alternatively, turn right and meander through the Forêt d'Orléans. There are a number of forest tracks, as well as waymarked paths and bridleways.

Sully, like Gien, was badly damaged during World War II but it has been carefully and thoughtfully restored. Fortunately, the fine château escaped serious damage. The château sits just off the River Loire, in a moat created by the River Sange. The main part of the building dates from the fourteenth century and it looks rather like a fortress. Joan of Arc visited the château in 1429, and again in 1430 when she was kept almost as a prisoner by the jealous La Trémoille, one of the King's favourites.

The château's most famous resident was Sully, originally Maximilien de Béthune and made Duc de Sully by Henri IV. He was one of Henri's key Ministers, restoring the finances and fortunes of France through sheer hard work. Sully made several changes to the château, including the addition of a seventeenth-century wing. Much of the château can be visited, including the upper part of the keep, which has one of the finest timber roofs in Europe. It is over 600 years old, yet looks almost new. This is chiefly due to the type of wood used (chestnut) and the craftmanship. Chestnut is not attractive to worms, so there is no rot; this, in turn, means there are no flies, and so no spiders or cobwebs.

The apartments in the château, like so many in the Valley, are scantily furnished. However, there is enough, plus the well-restored decorations, to enable the visitor to get a feel of life in previous times,

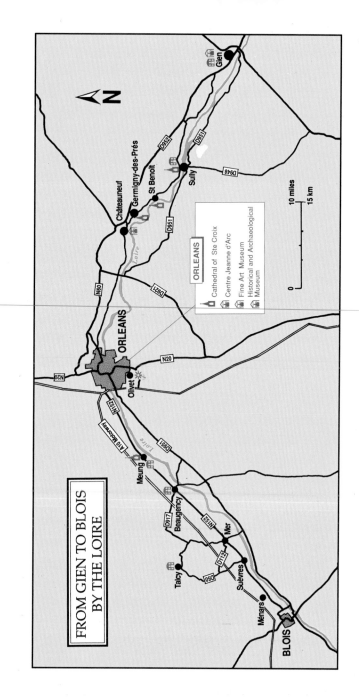

Gien

The château at Sully

when Voltaire was a regular visitor; he often wrote and performed plays here. Elsewhere in the town, the Collégiale de Saint Ythier (the collegiate church) is worth a visit to see its two fine examples of sixteenth-century stained-glass windows.

Cross (or re-cross) the River Loire to the far bank, and turn left on the D60 to **St Benoît.** This small village is home to one of France's finest Romanesque buildings. In fact, this place was a religious centre long before Christianity arrived. The early Gauls regarded this area as both the physical and spiritual centre of their territory. The Druids gathered here each year in conclave. It was inevitable that a Christian presence would eventually appear and a monastery was built here in the seventh century.

To enhance the monastery's prestige, the abbot arranged for the bodies of St Benedict (St Benoît) — founder of the Benedictine Order — and his sister St Scolastica to be brought from the ruined monastery at Monte Cassino. A 'strip-cartoon' in stone on the lintel of the north door of the basilica tells this story. The abbey now took the name of St Benoît.

Pilgrims and patrons came to the abbey and it became a famous centre of learning and teaching in both the sciences and the arts. Monks built roads and bridges, drained and farmed. So wealthy did the order become that, in order to transfer money safely from one place to another, it invented letters of credit. Louis VII borrowed money from the Benedictines to finance his disastrous Second Crusade of 1147.

During the Wars of Religion between Catholics and Protestants in the sixteenth century, the abbey was ransacked and its treasures either sold or melted down. Despite a revival in the seventeenth century, the Revolution eventually shut the abbey down. The church became a national monument in the mid-nineteenth century, and was steadily restored. Monks returned after the last war, and the Gregorian chant sung during services is a widely admired musical experience.

The church can be visited, as can the services of Mass or Vespers. The architecture is a beautiful, simple Romanesque, with vaulting and lovely sculpture on the porch and chancel capitals. The chancel floor has a Roman mosaic, which was brought from Italy. The crypt contains St Benedict's shrine.

The D60 continues out of St Benoît to **Germigny-des-Prés**, where there is a delightful ninth-century church in Byzantine style which contains a superb mosaic by the Ravenna School in the cupola of the east apse. There are 130,000 pieces of glass in the picture of the Ark of the Covenant flanked by angels. Continuing out of Germigny on the D60, the road arrives in **Châteauneuf-sur-Loire**.

Châteauneuf stands on the apex of a curve of the River Loire, facing the flat Sologne on the opposite bank, and with the Forêt d'Orléans to its rear. Like so many of the Loire crossing points, it suffered badly during World War II but has been graciously rebuilt. There are shady walks along riverside paths, a bathing beach and swimming pool, a covered market-place and street arcade.

The town no longer has a château but its park remains and is well-known for its rhododendrons and azaleas. The château's rotunda, which is now the Town Hall, contains the interesting Musée de la Marine de Loire. This tells the story of commercial boating on the Loire and the life of the boatmen, using photographs, models and various documents. From Châteauneuf it is only a short distance to one of the Loire Valley's key cities — Orléans.

Orléans has always played an important role in French history, and today it remains an administrative and business centre. The city was the capital of France under the Capetians in the tenth century, and the Duchy of Orléans traditionally went to the youngest branch of the reigning family. The city is best-known for its connections with Joan of Arc, who raised the siege by the English in 1429.

Joan, probably deceived by her advisers, arrived on the wrong side of the River Loire and had to send her troops back to Blois to cross. Meanwhile, she crossed upstream and arrived in Orléans the following day. Over the 4 days between 4 and 8 May 1429, Joan led a series of successful attacks, culminating in the relief of the city and the defeat of the English. This was a turning point in the Hundred Years War, and the future of England in Europe. The relieving of the siege is celebrated every year. Every 7 and 8 May the Joan of Arc Festival is held with panache, fervour and fireworks to honour the Maid who had instituted this thanksgiving for deliverance in 1430.

The wars in which Orléans has played its part have left their mark, and there is very little in the way of an old quarter. Despite its historical connections, Orléans is very much a city of today and as recently as the late 1970s one of the last main open areas — the Campo Santo, a medieval cemetery — was bulldozed to make room for a car park. Most of the historical interest lies around the cathedral, although the heart of the city is very much in the Place du Martroi, where the statue of Joan of Arc on her horse is situated.

A walk around the main places of interest could begin here. On the south side of the square is the eighteenth-century chancellory, restored after bombing in the last war. Alongside, on the other side of

A typical village street of the Loire

The mosaic inside the ninth-century church at Germigny-des-Prés

the Rue Royale, is a nineteenth-century copy of the chancellory, now the chamber of commerce. The Rue Royale, which runs down to the river, is one of the city's main shopping streets. From the Place du Martroi, take the Rue de la Hallebarde at the western corner, by the far end of the chancellory. This leads to Place Charles de Gaulle, where Joan of Arc's house is situated.

This half-timbered house, home of Jacques Boucher, is where Joan stayed in 1429, and is now the Centre Jeanne d'Arc, with a series of audio-visual presentations about Joan and Orléans. A little further off the square, in Rue du Tabour, is a museum tracing the life of Charles Péguy, the poet and philosopher. Cross the Rue Royale into Rue de Bourgogne, which is largely pedestrianised and has many shops. On reaching the Préfecture (previously a Benedictine monastery), turn left towards the cathedral. Notice the Salle des Thèses, which is opposite the Préfecture. This former library is all that remains of the university where Calvin studied. Rue Pothier leads to the Cathedral of Ste Croix.

Orléans Cathedral is very much a mixture of styles — in some respects reflecting the city itself. It was begun in the thirteenth century and rebuilt between the seventeenth and nineteenth centuries, supposedly in a Gothic style. The craftsmanship throughout is superb. It is possible to visit the crypt (where earlier remains of previous buildings are visible), and the treasury.

On the north side of the cathedral square is a Fine Arts Museum (Musée des Beaux-Arts), with an excellent series of galleries with works ranging from the fourteenth century to the present day. Around the corner from the museum, in Place de l'Etape, are some of the remaining old houses. Hôtel Groslot is a large Renaissance mansion, often used by the monarch. Incidentally, an *hôtel* in this context is best translated as a large town house. Opposite are the Pavillons d'Escures, pleasant town houses of the seventeenth century. Rue d'Escures leads back to Place du Martroi. The city's historical and archaeological museum is just off Rue Jeanne d'Arc and Rue Royale. It has a superb collection of Gallo-Roman items.

Orléans is a good base from which to explore the upper part of the Loire Valley. There are regular tours by coach. Alternatively, it is only a short train ride to Blois or Tours. Although the city centre has many hotels, drivers are likely to find the modern hotels south of the river more useful (especially as most have car parks). The southern suburbs of Orléans are very attractive as the key local industry is horticulture. On the tongue of land between Loire and Loiret is Faubourg St Marceau which provides the flowers that can be seen everywhere in Orléans. Its roses, in particular, are famous. Roses, as well as other plants, are grown in the Jardin Botanique in Quai de Prague. A rural atmosphere emanates from the tree-shaded, narrow road along the north bank of the Loiret where there are watermills, small pleasure craft, fishermen and graceful swans.

A little further south is **Olivet**. Here there are more nurseries and the Parc Floral de la Source, delightfully planted out with flowers in seasonal succession, together with trees and lawns. A miniature railway, a little zoo and a restaurant make the park a popular attraction.

The Loiret is a curious river. It emerges, fully grown, as it were, from a pool occupied by flamingoes and other birds in the Parc Floral to flow 13km (8 miles) into the Loire. Its actual source is at Bouteille, 26km (16 miles) away near St Benoît-sur-Loire, where it starts as a subterranean tributary of the Loire's bed before emerging from its pool at Olivet.

The Loire reaches its most northerly point at Orléans. It now turns south-westwards, hemming in the Sologne. It is possible to 'cheat' in travelling from Orléans, by picking up the A10 motorway. This runs parallel to the Loire as far as Tours. This may help those in a hurry but much would be missed. To keep close to the river, take the N152, which runs along the north bank of the Loire towards Beaugency. The GR3 long-distance path also follows the north bank here, often much closer than the road.

Meung-sur-Loire could also be called Meung-sur-Mauve because the stream, coming down off the Beauce, divides briefly into three at Meung before rejoining to flow into the Loire. Once it drove the many mills (a few are still working) that ground cereals grown on the Beauce plateau. One watermill, Le Grand Moulin, is an art gallery. Along the Quai du Mail is the stone statue of Jehan de Meung (1240-1305), native of this town. It was he who added 18,000 more stanzas to the already celebrated poem, *Le Roman de la Rose*, written 50 years earlier by Guillaume de Lorris. To the romantic and allegorical love verses of the original, Jehan added a penetrating satire on the philosophical conventions of his day, criticising both royalty and the church. He revealed himself as a Renaissance humanist in the Middle Ages; his influence on later writers was profound, for his verse was a prototype of character analysis dear to French writers.

Another poet, François Villon, was held captive in the Château de Meung from 1469 for 2 years and tortured before his release under the king's amnesty. In going round the well-furnished château the visitor will see the *oubliettes* where Villon languished. Rabelais also knew Meung and stayed at the Grand Cour at **St Ay**, 6km (4 miles) along the N152. The fountain there is known as Fontaine Rabelais. The Church of St Pilhard (eleventh to thirteenth centuries) is cruciform in shape, which is rare among Loire Valley churches.

Across the river is an ancient place of pilgrimage, **Cléry-St André**; the pilgrimage is still observed on 8 September and the following Sunday. In 1280, peasants found an oak statue of the Virgin. A small church was erected. The miraculous find drew huge numbers of pilgrims already on this route towards Compostela in Spain. It proved highly profitable locally until in 1428, during the Hundred Years' War, the Earl of Salisbury ordered the demolition of the church; only its square tower remains. A rather stark Gothic basilica replaced it, chiefly at the instigation of Louis XI who often stayed in the house (now a school) to the right of the church. He and his wife were buried at Cléry. His statue is an 1894 reproduction and it is also possible to see his private chapel, and the one used by his more amiable cousin, the Bastard of Orléans, who continued Joan's work of forcing the English out of France after her death. He, too, was buried here. The heart of Louis XI's son was placed under a slab to the right of the nave.

Huguenots destroyed the original oak statue of the Virgin and put up a replica in the sixteenth century. In the richly decorated Chapelle St Jacques are examples of the apparel and utensils carried by medieval pilgrims. The stalls and south door were donated by Henri II; they bear his royal initials and, flouting convention, those of his mistress, Diane de Poitiers. The names of important visitors to the basilica since 1325 are carved in the nave.

From Cléry take the D951 as far as La Croix Blanche and then the D19 across the river into **Beaugency**. There is a good view of this small and pretty town from the bridge. Until modern times the bridge was the only crossing point between Blois and Orléans, and so was regularly attacked. It was captured on four different occasions by the English in the Hundred Years War, before Joan of Arc finally relieved it. The château contains a collection of local costumes; the old castle keep (confusingly called in French the *donjon*) is massive, but is ruinous inside.

· The N152 continues towards Blois. There is another nuclear power station on the opposite bank. If you want to see this, cross over at Beaugency or take the D951 at Mer to St Laurent Nouan, and then follow the signs to the Centre Nucléaire. The observation platform at the Centre overlooks the complex; models and diagrams explain the working of the station. A more distant prospect of the Centre

Detail of the Town Hall doorway, Beaugency

Beaugency →

Nucléaire can be gained from the north bank by turning off the N152 at Mer and taking the little riverside road to Avaray (Louis XIII château). It goes on to **Tavers**, which is old and watered by resurgent streams and fountains; its vanished castle belonged to the English crown.

The D951 hugs the riverbank on the way to Blois and offers some pleasant views. The N152, on the opposite bank, stays slightly inland. From Mer or Suèvres it is posible to take a brief 16km (10 mile) detour inland to visit the Château of Talcy. Externally severe, inside it has the feel of a bourgeois household of 400 years ago. Its charm and interest is enhanced by the association of three poets with it. Ronsard stayed at the château and wrote love poems to the 15-year-old Cassandra, daughter of the owner. Agrippa d'Aubigné fell in love with the same owner's grand-daughter, dedicating his verses to her. Cassandra's great-grandson was the romantic poet Alfred de Musset. Talcy's greatest claim to historical fame is that in 1562 Catherine de Medici arranged a meeting of Protestant and Catholic leaders there, in her unavailing effort at reconciling their bitter differences.

After Suèvres there is another delightful château at **Ménars**. Originally built in 1637, it was acquired in 1760 by Madame de Pompadour. She added two wings and four pavilions and had the gardens laid out formally. The château commands a superb position over the Loire, looking towards Chambord; it is best appreciated from the opposite bank of the river. At the time of writing, the château itself is closed for restoration. After another few miles the town of Blois is reached.

2

FROM GIEN TO BLOIS THROUGH THE SOLOGNE

For those who want to follow a different route from Gien; who perhaps have visited Orléans, and so are less concerned about the upper end of the Valley, the routes through the Sologne are an interesting and unusual option. For those who keep to the river, a day touring the Sologne is essential, if only to appreciate the emptiness that can still be found in much of rural France. It is a flat, marshy region that was scarcely touched until 100 years ago. Efforts were made over the years to improve it — the Romans were the most successful before modern times. Monks built drainage systems, but often schemes simply faded away.

The Sologne covers about one million acres of heath and mere, threaded by deserted country lanes. The dark and cowering domestic architecture seems to hark back to isolation and self-sufficiency. However, it is an area with a feel all of its own, ideal for a rural holiday and perfect for walking or birdwatching. The Sologne differs geologically from the neighbouring lands. It is a region of poor soils which many generations have struggled to reclaim. It is neither a historical province nor a modern *département*; 'the land without a name', Alain-Fournier called it in his famous fantasy-novel, *Le Grand Meaulnes* (1913). It is a *petit pays* which nobody much wanted when the *départements* were created. In 1790 the bulk of the Sologne was given to Loir-et-Cher; the northern piece went to Loiret; the eastern remainder to Cher.

For a long time its ancient forests were almost impenetrable. Even the upheavals of the Hundred Years' War and the Revolution of 1789 scarcely penetrated this archaic and impoverished countryside,

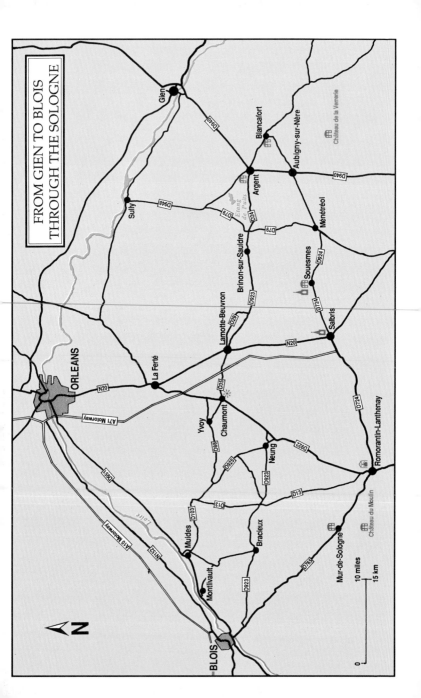

FROM GIEN TO BLOIS
THROUGH THE SOLOGNE

N

BLOIS

ORLEANS

A10 Motorway

A71 Motorway

LOIRE

Gien

Sully

Blancafort

Aubigny-sur-Nère

Château de la Verrerie

Argent

Ménétréol

Brinon-sur-Sauldre

Étang du Puits

Souesmes

Salbris

Lamotte-Beuvron

La Ferté

Chaumont

Yvoy

Neung

Romorantin-Lanthenay

Château du Moulin

Muides

Montlivault

Bracieux

Mur-de-Sologne

N20

D951

N152

D965

D103

D923

D13

D13

D922

D923

D765

D724

N20

D724

D724

D724

D924

D923

D79

D79

D948

D940

D940

D951

D922

D925

D98

D35

10 miles

15 km

Sologne cottages restored to their former glory

Aubigny-sur-Nère

better cultivated under the Romans than in the early nineteenth century. In the eleventh century some meres, or *étangs*, formed part of a drainage system under the auspices of monks from surrounding monasteries: Marmoutier, Pontlevoy, Fleury (St Benoît-sur-Loire), Selles-sur-Cher, St Aignan, and by the Counts of Blois and the Dukes of Orléans. The region was self-supporting, but then came neglect, rural exodus and endemic malaria. Not until a century ago did substantial improvements begin: creation of credit, reafforestation, large-scale agricultural co-operation and the introduction of new techniques and crops, drainage and marketing. More recently, new roads have opened up the Sologne to tourism, and an old and distinctive way of life and language has all but vanished.

Architectural traditions more or less mark out the limits of ethnic Sologne. Houses and farms were once low buildings of wood and cob (clay, gravel and straw); they gave way to equally low timber-framed and dark red herring-bone brick dwellings which are still widespread and characterise the region. They make a rough circle a little south of the great loop in the Loire and follow part of the Cher, turning north where the Sauldre enters the Cher.

From Gien it is a straight run on the D940 to **Argent-sur-Sauldre**, with its château and gardens overlooking the River Sauldre. East of Argent, by the D8, is Blancafort, with its pleasant pink brick fifteenth-century château. Also near Argent is one of the Sologne lakes, or meres — the Etang de Puits — which has been laid out for water-sports. From Argent the D940 heads south in a dead straight line to Bourges. About 10km (6 miles) down this road is **Aubigny-sur-Nère.**

In 1189 Aubigny (*Albiniacum* in Roman times) became part of the royal domain and prospered. Charles VII enlisted Scottish help against the English, and in 1423 gave Aubigny to John Stuart of Darnley, his Constable, in recognition of his services to the French king. A succession of distinguished Stuarts reigned at Aubigny until 1672 when the last male heir died. Although it reverted to Louis XIV, he gave it to Louise de Keroualle, Duchess of Portsmouth and mistress of England's Charles II. Aubigny was held by her descendants — the Dukes of Richmond — until 1834. Scottish artisans were brought over and industries such as glass-making and cloth-weaving flourished for 200 years.

Until the nineteenth century, the town was known as Aubigny-les-Cardeux or Carders. Numerous streets with early sixteenth-century houses survive. Their oak beams came from the Forêt d'Ivoy in which the Stuarts had their summer residence, the Château de la Verrerie — the Glassworks Château. This is as delightful as is its lakeside setting, 10km (6 miles) from Aubigny along the D89. It was given to the Stuarts by Charles VII, in addition to the town.

The Town Hall in Aubigny was once the château of the Stuarts. Next door are the graceful public gardens, Le Parc de la Duchesse de Portsmouth. The Stuart coat of arms can be seen on the Town Hall, the Maison du Bailli and the Church of St Martin. Three round towers down by the river are all that remain of the original ramparts.

From Aubigny it is possible to get an idea of the Sologne proper by heading towards Ménétréol and Souesmes. **Souesmes** was an important Roman crossroads. In addition to tenth-century remnants in its church, there are old houses and mills in and outside Souesmes (some are on the Pierrefitte-sur-Sauldre road). The Château de Souesmes (fourteenth to sixteenth centuries) has a central tower on its *motte* which serves as a staircase.

Due south for 9km (6 miles) on the D29 is the Radio-astronomy Observatory of **Nançay**, which has one of the largest radio-telescopes in the world. There are explanatory notices and tapes, and guided visits take place on the second Saturday of each month at 2.30pm by previous written arrangement. Nançay village contains artisans' studios whose collective works are exhibited at the Grenier de Villâtre.

The D724 from Souesmes runs to Salbris, which is on both the N20 and the A71 to Orléans. **Salbris**, like Souesmes, was an important Roman crossroads of the Orléans to Bourges and Blois to Bourges highways. The Church of St George has a pièta from the Abbaye St Sulpice in Bourges. The densest area of meres lies between the N20 and the Sologne's largest town, **Romorantin-Lanthenay**, which is only a short drive from Salbris.

Romorantin is the 'capital' of the Sologne and it lies on the River Sauldre. The town retains an interesting old quarter and has a number of old houses, primarily half-timbered. The Town Hall contains the fascinating Musée de Sologne which offers a detailed exposition of the Sologne, covering subjects ranging from geology to traditions. There are also two interiors of traditional cottages. The town also has a racing car museum, chiefly due to the fact that the car company Matra have a factory here.

All the lanes north of Romorantin lead through unspoilt countryside, and up towards the Loire again. Alternatively, two short itineraries from Romorantin reveal something of southern Sologne. First, the D59 to the west of the town brings you to one of the most agreeable of Sologne châteaux. Château du Moulin is 1.5km (1 mile) outside the village of Lassay-sur-Croisne. Built of red and black brick

A château near La Ferté

Château de la Verrerie

Attractive half-timbered buildings are widespread in the area

between 1480 and 1502 by Philippe de Moulin, it remains furnished in the style of his times. Make a point of seeing the vaulted kitchen and huge chimney, as well as the interior courtyard and its fifteenth-century well. A painting of the château as it was before the addition of the east tower is in the small fifteenth-century Church of St Denis in Lassay; there is also a fresco of St Christopher which dates from the end of the fifteenth century.

North of Lassay is **Mur-de-Sologne** whose sixteenth-century moated Château de la Morinière stands buried in woodlands. Take the Contres road as far as Soings-en-Sologne (Roman urns found here are in the museum at Blois, and a Roman statuette is displayed in Tours). Turn left onto the D119 and, just before Rougeou, turn right onto the D63. You come to **Chémery** whose Renaissance manor house is near the Etang de l'Arche.

A fairly narrow road west takes you past the sizeable Etang de Bonneuil to **Couddes** whose church has twelfth-century frescoes on the north wall of the nave, and fourteenth-century ones on the south wall. The theme of the former is St Christopher appearing before King Dannus, and the latter shows Christ in Majesty, angels of the Last Judgement and the Resurrection of the Dead. From Couddes, a gentle run along lanes leads to Méhers, Billy and Gy-en-Sologne where there is a museum of old agricultural implements, the Locature de la Straize. The return to Romorantin by D59 is a pretty route past some lakes. From Romorantin it is a straightforward drive along the D765 to reach Blois.

Those wanting to keep a more northerly route from Gien can still explore around Argent-sur-Sauldre, but rather than head south, take the D24 and D923 through Brinon-sur-Sauldre to Lamotte-Beuvron. Cross the N20 and take the D35 to **Chaumont-sur-Tharonne**. This small village stands on a raised motte, and was once surrounded by ramparts. These determined the village's layout, and can still be traced during a pleasant walk.

As at Romorantin, almost any road out of Chaumont-sur-Tharonne winds through delightful countryside. The D123 heads south through St Viâtre, past lakes and meres, to Selles and Romorantin. Heading westwards through Yvoy or La Marolle, more lakes and meres are visible until the edges of the Fôret de Boulogne and the Parc de Chambord are reached. The D103 and the D923 both skirt the edge of the park. The D103 joins the D951 to run along the south bank of the River Loire; the D923 joins the D765 towards Blois. Both routes run into Blois from the south, across the new bridge and into the town.

3
BLOIS AND CHAMBORD

B **lois** is one of the main centres for the visitor to the Loire Valley. As a town in its own right it holds plenty of interest, but it is also an ideal base from which to explore many of the well-known châteaux in the Valley. The town is built around the château, which is situated on a hill above the river. As a result, the streets and alleys are steep and not really suitable for vehicles. Fortunately, the town has recognised this, and much of the town centre is pedestrianised, which makes a visit even more pleasurable.

In the Middle Ages, Blois was the capital for the Counts of Blois, who were great rivals to the Counts of Anjou. The county was sold to the Duke of Orléans in the late fourteenth century and then passed to Charles d'Orléans, who began the gradual rebuilding of the château. Charles' son became King Louis XII and, like his father, had a great affection for the château, spending some time here. Louis was succeeded by François I, who added to the château. Throughout the sixteenth and seventeenth centuries the town and the château played their part in national life. It was only when Louis XIV became king, and moved the court to Versailles, that life began to pass the town by.

The château itself is highly recommended, regardless of the im- pression one gets from the exterior. The inner courtyard offers a fascinating glimpse of the styles of château building on each of the four sides. Although each occupant did some rebuilding, they retained much of what had gone before. As a result, it is possible to see and visit examples of building from the thirteenth to the seventeenth centuries. Enter the château from the Place de Château, which is usually full of coaches. Just before going into the entrance it is possible to make out the thirteenth-century hall which is alongside the fifteenth-century wing.

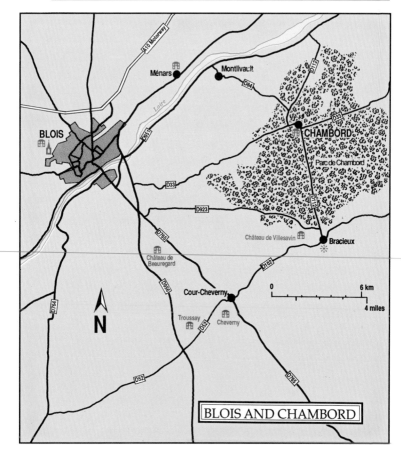

BLOIS AND CHAMBORD

Pass through the château's bookshop, and into the inner courtyard. Immediately in front is the Gaston d'Orléans wing (dating
from the seventeenth-century Classical period). To the left is the
Charles d'Orléans Gallery, with the late fifteenth-century chapel.
Immediately behind is the late fifteenth-century Louis XII wing. To
the right is the sixteenth-century François I wing, with its superb
staircase. It is possible to visit several of the apartments in the
François I wing which, though sparsely furnished, are very well-
decorated and maintained. There are two outstanding fireplaces, as
well as tapestries. The emblems of the famous royal residents are

The François I staircase, Château de Blois

everywhere, whether it is in the window glass or stone carving. There is a porcupine for Louis XII, a cord and ermine tails for Anne of Brittany and a salamander for François I. The visitor will also see their initials: L(Louis), A(Anne), F(François).

The visit also includes Catherine de Medici's panelled dressing room, complete with secret compartments, as well as several other rooms. One is where the Duc de Guise was assassinated in 1588, another contains Catherine de Medici's bed. The visit ends in the fourteenth-century Salle des Etats Généraux, a huge council hall where the States General (the French equivalent of the early English Parliament) met twice in the sixteenth century.

The château also contains a Fine Arts Museum on the first floor of the Louis XII wing (just to the right of the exit door); its contents are mainly portraits. When you have completed the château visit, it is worth visiting the bookshop and souvenir shop on the way out. There are some excellent books and information among the less endearing souvenirs. Overnight visitors to Blois, or those staying close by, may want to sample the *son-et-lumière* presentation that takes place in the courtyard during the summer. The Tourist Office can supply details and tickets.

By crossing the Place du Château to the far side, the visitor is provided with some fine views across the town to the Loire and beyond from the shady gardens. Steps lead down to the pedestrian precinct. A stroll around the picturesque streets of the old quarter is rewarding and there are many views of the well-restored, half-timbered houses and mansions. It is often possible to get a glimpse into the courtyards too. There are some good shopping streets which have colourful boutiques and, amid the older, high-sided alleys, there is the twelfth-century Church of St Nicholas. This has an impressive blend of architecture; its narrow nave and delicately carved apse are outstanding.

There are several routes which the tourist office (and local photographic shops) suggest. However, from the bottom of the steps from Place du Château, in Rue St Martin, it is possible to bear left and walk along Rue des Trois Clefs, where there are half-timbered houses, across Rue Denis Papin, up some steps, and along Rue Pierre de Blois. Numbers 1, 3, 6, and 8 are all of interest. This lane leads to the cathedral which was originally built in the sixteenth century but fell down and was rebuilt in the present Gothic style. Behind the cathedral is the Town Hall (formerly the Bishop's Palace), and some pleasant gardens with lovely views.

From the cathedral, cross the Place St Louis to the far right hand side. Alongside Rue Pierre de Blois, and spanning it with a wooden bridge, is a pleasant Gothic-style house. At the entrance to Rue du Palais, at No 3, is a half-timbered house which has carved posts with acrobats. Continue along Rue du Palais. On the left there is a good view from the steps (Escaliers Denis Papin); walk down the steps and bear left into Rue Haute. Continue into Rue des Juifs — numbers 6, 3, and 1 are all fine examples of town houses. At the little square, turn left into Rue du Puits Chatel. Most of the houses in this street are delightful examples of sixteenth-century residences. Turn right down Rue du Grenier à Sel into Rue Vauvert, where there is an old barn. As you reach Rue de la Fontaine des Elus, the fountain itself is on the left. However, turn right, and then left into Rue du Poids du Roi, recross Rue Denis Papin, and continue along Rue des Orfèvres back to Place Louis XII, at the foot of the château steps.

There are many other old houses to be discovered by wandering around the town. The Tourist Office also organises regular guided walking tours. Children may well put up with a walk around the town with the promise of a visit to the Poulain chocolate factory. Guided tours are available on weekdays, but do check arrangements with the Tourist Office in advance.

Blois is also an ideal base from which to visit some of the countryside châteaux. There are regular organised trips and the really adventurous can take a light aircraft or a helicopter trip around the better known châteaux. Anyone without transport would be better off choosing one of the many coach tours. These vary from a couple of hours to a full day, and the châteaux that are visited vary too. Visiting the châteaux needs careful planning — there are a lot of them, and very few are in a position where it is possible to drive past and just have a look. Chambord is one of the exceptions in this last category. Of all the Loire châteaux, Chambord and Chenonceau are probably the best-known but they couldn't be more different. Chambord is only a short distance from Blois.

Leave Blois by the new bridge. Either turn left just after the bridge on the D951, or continue a bit further and take the D33 which leads straight to Chambord. The D951 is a nicer route in many respects, albeit longer, as it runs alongside the Loire for much of the way. There is a good view of the Château de Ménars opposite. Turn right at Montlivault on to the D84, which runs to Chambord. When the road reaches the edge of the park, it passes through a wall. The wall is 32km (20 miles) long — the longest in France. It surrounds the whole 14,000 acre estate. Most of the estate is forested and it is a National Hunting Reserve.

Château Chambord

*The State apartments
at Château de Blois*

Troussay

Cheverny

The D84 comes to a crossroads where you should turn right. Follow the signs which bring you into the car park beside the château.

Chambord is the biggest Loire château, built to satisfy the mega-lomaniac desires of François I. Although its design is inherently feudal — there is a central keep and four corner towers — the flamboyance of its Renaissance styling is overwhelming.

François had it built after his return from Italy in 1519. Many architects and masons added to it but it was not finished by the time François died in 1557. A fortified hunting lodge of the Counts of Blois had stood on the swampy site. This was demolished and in its place had to go a château that was larger than anybody else's. A few statistics give an idea of the vast ambition: 156m by 117m (512ft by 384ft), flanked by six massive towers; 440 rooms; 14 main staircases, 70 secondary ones; 800 capitals; 365 chimneys. Teams of hundreds of workmen were drafted to build the cheerless folly. The façade is an enormous film-set extravaganza; the interior impresses by its extraordinary staircases and there is a forest of sculpted chimneys. A walkway round the château offers a panorama of the park.

François was a keen hunter; Chambord was his fantastical hunting lodge where he entertained lavishly. However, the place was uncomfortable and never properly lived in. Various kings paid brief visits; Molière performed two plays there in the presence of Louis XIV, and Louis XV was the last royal resident. Every owner wanted to be rid of it and, eventually, the State bought it in 1930.

The interior of Chambord contains some furniture and trophies, and the decoration is impressive. The most striking aspects are the staircase (a double spiral which never meets), and the panoramic terrace with a multitude of chimneys, windows and spires. It is possible to walk around the gardens and exterior without paying, and this can be a more rewarding experience which allows the visitor to appreciate the vast scale of the place.

Chambord is where the idea of *son-et-lumière* was first conceived, in the 1950s. Along with many other châteaux, it continues this new tradition. It is worth checking with local tourist offices for details of costs, length of performance and subject.

South from Chambord, the D112 slices through the Parc de Chambord and Forêt de Boulogne to Bracieux, a distance of 8km (5 miles). **Bracieux** lies on the fringe of the Sologne and is a pleasant old town on the banks of the Beuvron which is crossed by a charming bridge. A sixteenth-century covered market is surmounted by a tithe-barn.

Turn right and follow the Beuvron. A couple of miles further on is

Ponts d'Arian. The village lies on the Roman road which came from Chartres. Cross the river to reach the small and modest Château de Villesavin, built in 1537 by François I's financial secretary who was in charge of paying for the building of Chambord. Erected by Italian workers employed on Chambord, Villesavin is very much an Italian Renaissance creation and this is emphasised by the Carrara marble used in it. The kitchens are of interest, and there is a display of horse-drawn vehicles as well as some rather dilapidated frescoes. Note the pigeon-loft, complete with its revolving ladder. The loft was for 1,500 pigeons: a precise figure because of the legal nicety which stated that an owner was allowed one pigeon to every acre in his possession; any more would annoy the neighbours.

Return to Ponts d'Arian and turn right on to the D102 for Cour-Cheverny. On the far side of the village is another celebrated château; **Cheverny**. Its harmonious unity of style was achieved because the dignified white tufa-stone building was put up to an unaltered plan in 30 years, between 1604 and 1634. It has never been altered or had its façade cleaned because the tufa whitens with age. The tour includes the handsomely proportioned and well-furnished rooms; the King's Room is the most striking; the Grand Salon has paintings by Titian, Mignard and of the School of Raphael.

Outside, the pack of hounds in their kennels can be seen, as can the Hunting Museum which has 2,000 pairs of antlers. Meets are held twice a week in winter when the huge, ornate coiled horns (the Trompes de Cheverny) pierce the air with their high-pitched sound. As the extensive grounds are not open to the public, you can do no more than glimpse the handsome trees through the railings.

Four kilometres (3 miles) further west is the small Renaissance *gentilhommière* (manor house) of **Troussay**, restored in the nineteenth century. The owner brought various items to the château such as sculptures, windows or flagstones from various monuments in the district which have now disappeared. Outbuildings by the court-yard house collections of old agricultural implements and domestic utensils of yesteryear.

Continue west from Troussay until you hit the D956 going north. Beyond Cellettes, on the right, is **Beauregard**. This modest and el- egant building, more a manor house than a château, had been the home of Jean de Thiers, minister under Henri II, and friend of Ronsard. The visit is made more interesting by virtue of the gallery of 363 portraits of people who were well-known in the late sixteenth century. From Château de Beauregard and back to Blois is a distance of 7km (5 miles) through the Forêt de Russy.

4
FROM BLOIS TO TOURS

T hose seeking to reach the city of Tours quickly can take the A10 motorway. If you are using the main towns as a base from which to explore, this may be the best option. Those happy to take a little longer and experience some of the countryside can again follow either side of the Loire. The N152 follows the north bank, the D751 the south. On this occasion, the former route is preferable, as there are opportunities to dip into the Forêt de Blois (all that is left of the huge broad-leaf forests that once covered this area). Beyond the forest there is good farmland which is also suitable for vineyards because the land rises steadily as it gets further from the river.

There is plenty of interest in **Mesland** besides its wines. It was known as Fontaine-Mesland until the middle of the eighteenth century because its fountain was thought to possess healing properties. All manner of Gallo-Roman finds testify to the antiquity of the place, and the general view is that Mesland derives from *Hermèslande* (Hermes Heath), Hermes having been a Romanised Gaulish god, the horned *Cernumnus*. The porch of the Romanesque church of 1060 has twenty-six stylised, helmeted and bearded heads. These are very reminiscent of Gaulish carvings of head-hunting warriors in the museums of Aix-en-Provence and Marseille. Inside the church are twelfth-century fonts, a Virgin and Child of the thirteenth century, and another of the sixteenth century from the Abbey of Marmoutier.

From Mesland the D1 leads to Onzain, and then back to the N152. While this road has run alongside the Loire from Blois, it is busy and those seeking a quieter route might prefer to follow the D58. This traces the line of the River Cisse, running parallel to the Loire. Whichever route is used, make sure the river is crossed to reach **Chaumont**. In fact, the location of the château is best appreciated

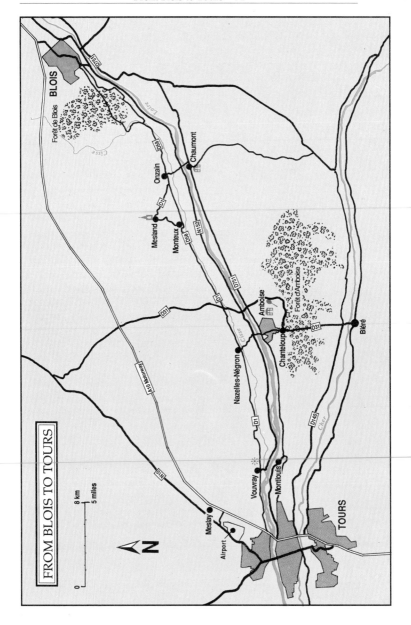

from the far bank. However, there are no lay-bys, traffic is heavy, and the next bridge is at Amboise, so save the view for after the château visit.

Chaumont's position dominates this stretch of the Loire. The château sits in handsome confidence on the highest spur of rock along the banks of the river. From the village — just one long street — the climb is quite an effort. High-walled, with massive round white towers and pepperpot roofs, Chaumont was built in the late fifteenth and early sixteenth centuries on the site of much earlier castles. Looking more medieval than Renaissance, the exterior is the most worthwhile part of a visit. This is not only because of its splendid appearance but also for the views from the eighteenth-century terrace, for its grounds with ancient cedar trees, and its spacious stables put up in 1877.

Compared with others, the château at Chaumont has had a relatively peaceful history. Its chief notoriety is that Catherine de Medici gave it to her late husband's mistress, Diane de Poitiers, in exchange for Chenonceau. Diane did not relish the arrangement and soon abandoned Chaumont for her château at Anet. The interior of Chaumont was transformed and modernised at crippling expense from 1875 onwards until financial disaster hit the owners. It has been State-owned since 1938. If the interior is less interesting than the outside, there are still some tapestries, terracotta medallions, Renaissance furniture, and the rooms of the two rivals, Catherine and Diane, to be seen.

Go back across the bridge, and turn left along the north bank of the river towards Amboise (on the N152). This gives an excellent view of the château's position over Chaumont village; as well as offering a fine view of the château at Amboise. Most of Amboise lies on the south bank of the river, so cross at the bridge (from which there is another good view of the town). There is ample car parking in the town.

Amboise is similar to Blois because it has retained a great deal of its character. Much of the town centre is pedestrianised and there is a good choice of both hotels and restaurants.

The visitor is offered plenty of distractions: the *son-et-lumière* performance, *Soirée à la Cour du Roy* at the château in July and August is a spectacle of local dancers, riders and jugglers. There are concerts; wine fairs in April and August; Sunday morning markets and wine *caves*. In high summer, guided tours of the town are available. Outdoor activities include cycling, walking, riding, tennis, swimming (open-air and covered pools), fishing and watersports. There are campsites on the Ile d'Or and outside Amboise; holiday camps; youth hostels and various types of letting accommodation.

Beginning as a township of wooden houses and palisades founded by the Carnutes, it attracted the eye of Caesar's lieutenant Crassus who made it his winter quarters and named it *Ambacia* after the little tributary La Masse which flows into the Loire to the south. It is said that the Roman walls were still standing in 1646 where Place St Denis is now. The caves below the plateau on which the château stands have been called 'Caesar's granaries', and wheat may well have been stored in them.

Amboise was the meeting place of Clovis, king of the Franks, and Alaric II, king of the Visigoths, in AD503. During Viking invasions, the people of Amboise were massacred at Négron. However, history centres itself chiefly on the château where two earlier medieval castles had stood; a third had been in the town lower down. Charles VIII and his wife Anne of Brittany began rebuilding the château in 1492. He was clearly a young man of taste, vision and impatience. Workmen had to labour day and night whatever the weather. Two years later, he campaigned in Italy. Dazzled by the richness of its art, Charles transferred to Amboise booty, artists, craftsmen, scientists and gardeners of Renaissance Italy; 'this terrestrial paradise', as he called it. This was the start of the Italian Renaissance influence in France. He had the formal garden at Amboise laid out in Italian style. What is visible now of the château is only a fragment (but a fine one) of the original.

François I arrived at Amboise at the age of 6 to complete an all-round education. The first 3 years of his reign were spent here creating a brilliant, diverse and stimulating life at court. He finished the wing of the palace begun by Louis XII. François' great love of the arts led him to try to persuade Michelangelo to come to France, but without success. He had more luck with Leonardo da Vinci, who came in 1516, and spent his last years nearby at Le Clos-Lucé. As François built new palaces closer to Paris, the Italian influence spread, and Amboise reached its most expansive point as a château.

In 1560, during François II's reign, a misconceived Protestant plot was uncovered, and the participants were killed at the château, apparently in the presence of the king's wife; Mary, Queen of Scots. After this, Amboise went into a long decline. It passed to the rebellious Gaston d'Orléans, Louis XIII's brother and, during one of his uprisings, royal troops demolished much of the outer defences. Louis XIV regained Amboise and turned it into a prison. After the French Revolution, with no money for its upkeep, more of the

Château d'Amboise

buildings were demolished. Bombing damaged even more during World War II. Only one wing, less than one-fifth of the château, remains, although it is enough to give an impression of what the building was like when intact. The lavish *son-et-lumière* presentation during the summer enhances the atmosphere.

The entrance to the château is by a steep ramp from Rue Victor Hugo, which leads to a terrace overlooking the Loire. The visit takes in all the key remaining buildings including the Logis du Roi (Royal Apartments), St Hubert's Chapel, the Tour Heurtault, and the famous Tour Minimes. This contains a ramp up which horses and coaches could come from the town below. Return to the town down the ramp. Crossing Rue Victor Hugo allows the visitor to explore the town centre. There is a pretty clock tower, and philatelists will find the Postal Museum, in Rue Joyeuse, of great interest.

Returning to Rue Victor Hugo, follow the road uphill, away from the river. About 1km ($^1/_2$ mile) along, on the right, is Le Clos-Lucé, where Leonardo da Vinci lived from 1516 until his death in 1519. Parking is very limited at the roadside, so it is best to leave the car in the town and walk. Le Clos-Lucé was acquired in 1490 by Charles VIII, and is a delightful red brick manor house. Unlike many of the

Street scene, Amboise

châteaux, it is on a more human scale and is easier for the visitor to relate to. Entry to the pleasant gardens is free; there is a charge to visit the house and the exhibition of Leonardo's inventions.

The house itself has been very well-restored, and is worth visiting. It has been well-furnished with period furniture, including three eighteenth-century rooms. The whole place has a homely feel to it, made more so by the various things on show that Leonardo had collected while staying there. Behind the house is a modern exhibition hall. This contains an audio-visual presentation about Leonardo and his work; and a fascinating exhibition of models of his inventions (including, for example, the aeroplane, the tank, the helicopter, the parachute, and the car). These have all been made by IBM engineers from the original drawings, using period materials. The gardens make for a useful pause, before returning back into the town.

South of Amboise is the lake-studded Forêt d'Amboise where Valois kings once hunted. If you take the D61 south-east you come to Bois de la Moutonnerie where there are signposted walks. The D31 out of Amboise brings you, in 2.5km ($1^1/_2$ miles), to a right turn to the Pagoda of Chanteloup. It is a folly, all that remains of Château de Chanteloup, built by the Duc de Choiseul in 1771. He had been Chief Minister to Louis XV but was banished to his château for having displeased Madame du Barry. A later Duc de Choiseul, Jean-Antoine Chaptal, chemist and minister under Napoleon, immortalised his own name in chaptalisation, the process by which sugar is added to wine to strengthen it. The château was pulled down in the last century. The 44m (144ft) high folly is beside a pool; you can climb to the top and see the forest stretched out below.

Returning to Amboise, a straightforward left turn on to the D751 makes for an easy run along the banks of the Loire into the heart of Tours. Alternatively, cross the Loire in Amboise but, rather than take the N152, continue straight on to Nazelles-Négron. Turn left onto the D1 to follow the pretty Cisse Valley to **Vouvray**. Vouvray is a wine-lover's paradise — there are plenty of *caves* in which to taste and buy. However, it is worth taking or consulting a good wine guide — most of the vineyards are small and quality can vary but it is possible to discover an outstanding wine. Vouvray produces a delightful sparkling *vin mousseux*, and is classified *Appellation Contrôlée*. From Vouvray it is only a short way along the Loire's north bank to reach Tours. Cross the river to get into the city centre.

5

TOURS, CHENONCEAU
AND LOCHES

T ours is the biggest city in the Loire Valley, after Angers. For many tourists it is the central base from which they will visit the Valley. It is easily reached from Paris: there are regular railway services, including the TGV (high speed) train. The A10 motorway cuts right through the city, from north to south. Inevitably, such an important centre has a long history, and a busy contemporary life. Like any big city nowadays, much of Tours is concrete and glass — chiefly the former — but the centre and the old quarters have survived, and have recently been through a prolonged restoration project.

For the visitor, the city has hotels of every grade and style, and attractions of all kinds as diversions from sightseeing. There are fairs and festivals, including a major music festival; theatre; outstanding sports facilities including swimming, riding and golf; cinemas; and just about everything you would expect to find in one of France's major cities. There are regular coach tours to the surrounding châteaux. The helpful tourist office, by the railway station, is well-staffed and equipped to deal with enquiries of every sort.

Tours was a significant early settlement, but really only grew in importance from the fourth century. This was as a place of pilgrimage to honour St Martin, one of the early bishops. Gregory of Tours enhanced the city's reputation as a place of learning and, in the eighth century, Charlemagne bought Alcuin of York to Tours as Abbot. However, the Norman invasions and the constant bickering between Blois and Anjou took their toll. Fortunes rose again during the fifteenth and sixteenth centuries, when the silk industry was

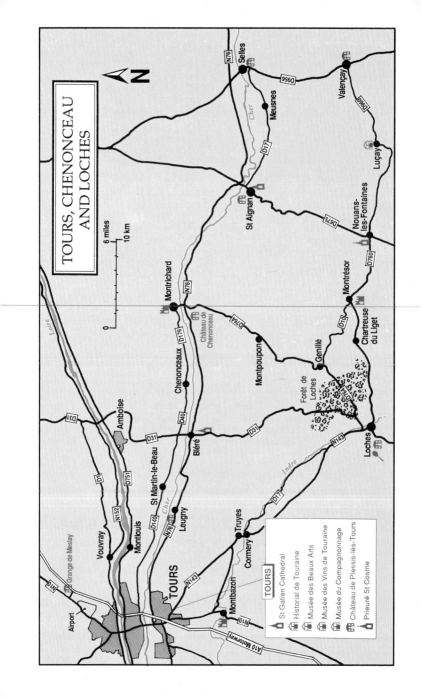

Place Plumereau, Tours

introduced. As a major city and intellectual centre, Tours became a base for Protestantism. The result of this was a massacre by Catholics in 1572, and this in turn led to an economic decline which was not reversed until the railways arrived in the nineteenth century. Since then, though, Tours has expanded, and today boasts a wide range of industries.

The city suffered badly during World War II. An overall restoration, focusing in particular on the damage to the old quarter around Place Plumereau, has only recently been completed. This has been a great success, and it is a real pleasure to wander around the streets, breathing in the atmosphere and window shopping.

The 'centre' of Tours is the Place Jean Jaurès, in which the huge ✳ Town Hall stands. Rue Nationale, the main north-south road, runs northwards to, and across, the Loire from here. To the right runs Boulevard Heurteloup, which passes the Tourist Office and the main railway station. Rue Nationale is very much the main shopping street in Tours — it is lined with well-known shops, boutiques and stores. About two-thirds of the way up Rue Nationale is a crossroads where the old main road once ran before the Pont Wilson was built. To the right is Rue Colbert, which leads to the château and the cathedral. It is also one of the best places for eating and entertainment.

Follow Rue Colbert and look out for the half-timbered house at number 41 and the sign '*A la Pucelle armée*' (To the armed Maid — ie: Joan of Arc). It was here that the craftsman who made Joan of Arc's armour lived. Continue along Rue Colbert to Rue Lavoisier, where a left turn leads to the château. It is worth starting a visit to Tours here, at the Historial de Touraine. This well-laid out waxworks museum, housed in what is left of the château, tells the story of the area in a series of tableaux, featuring the key events and figures of the Valley. A handy English language leaflet explains the different scenes.

Return up Rue Lavoisier to the cathedral. St Gatien's was built between the thirteenth and sixteenth centuries — the result is a harmonious mixture of Gothic, Flamboyant and Renaissance styles. Stained-glass windows flood the interior with glowing light. Visits can be made to the top of the south tower. Next door is the choir-school, La Psalette, another elegant construction of the fifteenth and sixteenth centuries.

South of the cathedral is the Musée des Beaux-Arts (Fine Arts Museum) in the former palace of the archbishop. Near the entrance is a small round tower, a late Gallo-Roman fragment of the defence walls of *Caesaródunum*. Scattered at random round the halls of the museum are some important paintings including ones by Rubens, Rembrandt, two Mantegnas and Jean Fouquet (a native of Tours). Later artists such as Degas, Delacroix, Nattier are also represented and there are works by sculptors including Bourdelle, Houdon and the local Sicard. Some rooms are decorated with Tours silks. These were produced in the fifteenth and sixteenth centuries from some of the 2,000 looms which required 20,000 workers.

Retrace Rue Colbert to find, on the right, the picturesque Place Foire-le-Roi. Medieval food markets were held here under the protection of the king. Trestles were converted into a stage for the presentation of open-air mystery plays. One of the old houses in Rue Colbert is Hôtel Babou de la Bourdaisière (No 8). This dates from 1520 and in the courtyard are three fourteenth-century arches transferred from the Augustinian cloisters.

Eglise St Julien, founded by Gregory of Tours, still retains fragments from the eleventh-century building; the rest dates from the twelfth and thirteenth centuries, but the stained-glass windows are modern. Following the bombing of 1940, the church cellars were rediscovered. Now the great vaults are hosts to a splendidly catholic

Musée des Vins de Touraine. Not only is it a history of wine-making, but also of the relationship between wine and human societies.

No less fascinating is the Musée du Compagnonnage, entered at 8 Rue Nationale, a history of craft guilds from the fifteenth century on. Tools and fine examples of work in different trades are on show. Documents are displayed which relate to the nationwide organisation whose members were persecuted by larger, existing unions and forced to meet in secret. It is worth coming to Tours just to see these two illuminating exhibitions.

Vieux Tours lies west of Rue Nationale. Approach it by Rue du Commerce, the extension of Rue Colbert. At No 25 is the lovely Renaissance Hôtel Gouin, whose elegant façade is delicately carved with floral motifs and coats of arms. Inside is the Musée de la Société Archéologique de Touraine whose chief exhibits are of medieval and Renaissance art, though archaeology also figures prominently.

Place Plumereau is at the heart of medieval Tours. All around are brick and timber gable-ended houses. Most have been carefully restored following the damage done during World War II.

The many cafés and restaurants in the square come to life in the evenings, when there is often street entertainment. The little streets and alleys of the old quarter are best explored and discovered at random. However, the Tourist Office hires out audio cassette guides to the old quarter, as well as offering guided tours.

Slightly further afield from the town centre, but still within present day Tours, and well worth a visit, are three places of particular interest. About 11km (7 miles) to the north — take the N10 across Pont Wilson, and continue past the airport and motorway turnings — is the Grange de Meslay. Originally a fortified farm belonging to Marmoutier Abbey, the superb tithe barn is one of the finest surviving medieval examples of its kind, chiefly due to the chestnut timberwork in the roof. A major music festival is held here in the summer.

To the west of Tours city centre, and reached by continuing along the south bank of the Loire from Pont Wilson for about 3km (2 miles), then following the signs, is the pretty Prieuré de St Cosme. Little remains of the buildings that the poet Ronsard would have known when he was prior here. However, the Prior's House still stands — it is a pleasant fifteenth-century building and contains a museum about Ronsard and his life. Ronsard's grave is also in the grounds.

A little further south-east (follow the railway line from St Cosme, then turn left at the signpost) is the Château de Plessis-lès-Tours. The rather grand name belies a modest fifteenth-century brick building

Château Chenonceau

which is all that remains of Louis XI's favourite château. There is a display about his life and it is possible to visit the room in which he died.

Tours does not just stand astride the Loire; the River Cher also runs through the city. Indeed, the Indre also sweeps up to almost reach the city boundaries, before turning westwards at Montbazon.

The Cher and the Loire seem barely able to part company until they begin to drift apart east of Tours, beyond the suburb of St Avertin whose leisure complex uses the Cher. St Avertin owes its name, it seems, to a Scottish monk of the twelfth century who withdrew to the then-lonely spot and died there. In June 1940, Château de Cangé at St Avertin saw the meeting between Winston Churchill and the French government, prior to the Franco-German armistice.

Beyond Tours, roads run each side of the Cher, though mostly at some distance from it. The road north of the river, D140, takes you to **St Martin-le-Beau** which produces a good white wine, but wine connoisseurs will have turned left earlier, setting their sights on **Montlouis-sur-Loire**. It lies almost opposite Vouvray, though there is no road bridge over the Loire to link the two wine towns anywhere between Amboise and Tours.

At Montlouis, vines of the Chenin grape cover the south-facing

❅

← *Half-timbered buildings in Tours*

83

outcrop on which the village is built. Wine can be bought at the co-operative or, for better quality, at private *caves*, many carved out of the chalk. On the quayside, the Renaissance *hôtel*, now a small museum, is the birthplace of the sixteenth-century printer, Christophe Plantin, whose serif typeface is still widely used.

The road along the south bank, the N76, passes St Avertin to Véretz and Azay-sur-Cher. Three kilometres (2 miles) south are some picturesque Romanesque remnants of the Prieuré St Jean-du-Grais. Château de Leugny is 1km ($^1/_2$ mile) out of Azay along the N76. **Leugny** overlooks the river, and the chief interest is the Louis XVI furniture.

Next comes the township of **Bléré** with 4,000 inhabitants, facing La Croix-en-Touraine on the other side of the Cher. Once known as *Briotreis*, Bléré was a parish founded by St Brice who succeeded St Martin as Bishop of Tours. The Church of St Christophe was built at different times, the nave being the oldest, perhaps dating from the tenth century. In the Place de la République is a domed funerary chapel (1526), Gothic in style but Italian Renaissance in its elegant detail.

The N76 continues through fields to a left turn, then over a bridge to Chenonceaux village, and the **Château de Chenonceau** (without the 'x'). Crossing the bridge offers a tantalising glance of what is to come. Of all the Loire châteaux, this is the most impressive — few would dispute that — and understandably popular. Even out of the main season it is always busy and it is best to arrive just as it opens, or shortly before it closes, for a less crowded view. Fortunately, the château and its grounds are efficiently run.

It is possible to wander at one's leisure. There is no obligatory guided tour as at so many châteaux, there is a pleasant souvenir shop, a tea-room and snack bar, as well as a small waxworks museum of the major figures in the history of the château. In the summer there is also a children's crèche, and boat trips along the river (if the water level allows). The enduring impression of Chenonceau is one of grace and harmony, of both architecture and setting.

Aux Temps des Dames de Chenonceau is the title of the *son-et-lumière* show in the gardens. The title emphasises the role of women in the château's history. It was built between 1513 and 1521 by Thomas Bohier, chamberlain to four kings. He acquired the property — then a modest working mill — by underhand means for next to nothing.

Bohier's duties for the king, François I, kept him away from Chenonceau for much of the time. So it was his wife, Catherine Briçonnet, who supervised the improvements. Bohier died in Milan in 1524, Catherine 2 years later, heavily in debt. In discharge of the debts, the king acquired Chenonceau. When Henri II inherited it, he gave it to his mistress, Diane de Poitiers. She spent 9 years completing the formal gardens, today called Le Jardin de Diane de Poitiers. Diane also had the arched bridge built over the River Cher, extending the main château building.

On Henri II's death, his wife, Catherine de Medici, was able to extract her perfect revenge on the mistress by forcing Diane to give up Chenonceau for Chaumont. Catherine spent a lot of time at Chenonceau, building the gallery over the bridge. She organised great parties and festivals at the château, and remodelled some of the grounds. On Catherine's death the château passed to her daughter-in-law, Louise de Lorraine, wife of Henri III.

After her husband had been assassinated, Louise retreated into Chenonceau and for 11 years wore the white robes of mourning; she became a wraith-like figure spoken of as La Dame Blanche.

When the Bourbon court gave up using the royal châteaux of the Loire and moved to Versailles, Chenonceau entered a period of neglect. It was bought by Claude Dupin in 1730. Again, a woman's influence was crucial to Chenonceau's fortunes. After Dupin's death, his wife held intellectual court there: Voltaire, Buffon the naturalist and Montesquieu the political philosopher were some of the great men of the day to stay there. Jean-Jacques Rousseau was engaged as tutor to Madam Dupin's child in 1746-7. Rousseau was to write later that he enjoyed his period at Chenonceau more than any other in his life.

Madame Dupin survived the Revolution, as did her château, through the loyal protection of the people in the vicinity. She lived to be 93. Her descendants sold Chenonceau in 1864, and another woman, Madame Pelou, dedicated herself to its restoration. The work of conservation has been continued by the present owner, Madame Menier. *Aux Temps des Dames de Chenonceau* is as apt a title for the *son-et-lumière* show today as it was 400 years ago. The entrance to the château is along an avenue of plane trees. The avenue opens out, with former stables and outbuildings (now the tea rooms and waxworks) on the right, and the entrance to Diane de Poitier's garden on the left. Across a drawbridge there is a large terrace with the keep of the original château. Cross the next bridge to enter the château itself.

Although there is no formal guided tour as such, visitors are guided around the château by a series of arrows. The rooms are well-signed (in English), and guide booklets are also available. Almost

Montrichard

every room has something of interest — too much to detail here — but look out for the little chapel, the great gallery over the Cher with its long, black and white floor, a superb drawing room, and the former kitchens inside one of the piers. A visit is nicely rounded off by a walk around the gardens, offering plenty of opportunities for the keen photographer. Chenonceau merits a morning or an afternoon at least, and those seeking a pleasant day out from Tours could combine Chenonceau with a visit to Amboise.

Chenonceau and Chambord are often described as the two 'great' Loire châteaux, at least in architectural terms. There is little doubt which is most people's favourite. Chenonceau is more popular, not only because of its perfect location, but because it is on a more human scale.

Anyone who has spent the morning at Chenonceau, and now wants to eat, is best advised to avoid the village itself. Instead, follow the Cher further east to Montrichard. At **Chissay en Touraine**, west of Montrichard on the north bank, is the Distillerie Fraise d'Or, where the unusual local strawberry liqueur can be purchased.

On the south bank, the lesser road leads straight to the bridge across the Cher to provide an attractive view of old **Montrichard** clustering round church and keep. Good hotels, restaurants and recreational facilities make Montrichard (population 3,800) worth visiting. The ruined square keep was started by Foulques Nerra in the tenth century; Richard Coeur-de-Lion was locked up for a while in the tiny cell at its foot. From the top, the town's roofs and church jumble below eye-level; beyond is the river and the distant countryside. A number of fine old houses from between the twelfth and sixteenth centuries survive, as well as some troglodyte dwellings around the keep. The twelfth-century church saw the pathetic wedding ceremony between 14-year-old Louis d'Orléans and Louis XI's 12-year-old daughter, Jeanne-de-France. Hunchbacked, crippled and facially deformed, she became a woman of noble character despite her physical afflictions. The town has a delightful park beside the river, complete with swimming pool and bathing area; it is ideal for a picnic.

Just outside Montrichard is Nanteuil Church (dating from the twelfth and thirteenth centuries) whose corbels of the nave vaults are handsomely carved with human faces; the two-storeyed Lady Chapel was built by Louis XI.

Montrésor

St Aignan is another pretty Touraine village on the south bank of the Cher. Its château rises impressively on a hill and is seen most photogenically from across the river. Old streets wind up to the château which is reached by a great sweep of steps. Only the terrace of the château can be visited; the view from it is admirable. Down the hill, where there are beam-and-plaster houses, is the early Gothic church whose crypt has frescoes from the twelfth to fifteenth centuries; one of the oldest is most impressive, a Christ in Majesty.

To the north of St Aignan is the graceful Manoir de Beauregard (by the D675 to St Roman-sur-Cher and right), skirting the Forêt de Gros-Bois. A little to the east, on the quiet D17, is **Meusnes.** This small village has an interesting museum in the Mairie, devoted to flint-locks and flint-knapping. For 300 years muskets were fired by means of flints, and the industry reached its apogee in the eighteenth century. To supply the army's needs, 500 knappers were kept fully employed to supply the 50 million flints used annually after the Napoleonic wars, as well as for export to Africa and Latin America. Professional knapping died out in France with World War I.

Just a little further, and back on the Cher, is **Selles-sur-Cher**. It has an interesting château on the banks of the river — pleasant seventeenth-century buildings hide a small park and forbidding remains of a solid thirteenth-century castle. Selles is only a short distance from Romorantin-Lanthenay, in the Sologne.

Plenty of roads run southwards from the Cher Valley. Most of the major ones run to the south-west towards Loches. From Selles, though, it is a short run south, along the D956, to Valençay. This is more of a palace than a château and is a little like Chambord. Built in 1540 by a *nouveau riche* financier, Jacques d'Estampes, its ostentatiousness appealed to its subsequent owners, almost all of whom were also financiers.

In 1803, Talleyrand (1754-1838) acquired the property. He was Abbot of St Denis, Bishop of Autun and Prince of the Empire under Napoleon whom he plotted to remove in favour of Murat. Talleyrand was also head of a provisional government shortly before Napoleon abdicated and intriguer *par excellence* under the Restoration. He was altogether the great political survivor.

Talleyrand entertained in high style at Valençay which consists of two ornamented wings at right angles to one another. The west wing is furnished in Empire style, and includes the 'Congress of Vienna' table and mementoes of the great man. A Talleyrand museum is lodged in an outbuilding. The formal gardens contain various animals and birds which roam freely; llamas and flamingoes are the most striking of these. Some sixty vintage cars dating from 1898 onwards, all in working order, can be seen in the Musée de l'Automobile du Centre in the château grounds. *Son-et-lumière* performances are weekend features in summer.

From Valençay it is possible to return to Tours by retracing one's route along the Cher. Alternatively, take the D960 to **Luçay**, to begin a pleasant cross country route to Loches. Luçay, like Meusnes, has a small flintlock museum — Musée de la Pierre à Fusil. From Luçay continue on the D960 and then the D760 to Nouans-les-Fontaines, to meet the D675, which is the road running down from St Aignan. The church in this tiny village contains an outstanding pièta behind the high altar.

The D760 is very pretty here and runs alongside a small river, the Indrois, as far as **Montrésor**. Montrésor is as delightful as its name suggests. Within the old castle defences — which is all that is left of Foulques Nerra's castle — is a pretty fifteenth-century château. It was restored by a polish count; the interior is as he left it and contains many souvenirs of his time there. From Montrésor there is a choice of two routes to Loches. The first follows the delightful Indrois Valley to Genillé, to meet the D764 from Montrichard. The second is to continue on the D760 direct to Loches. This route passes through the Forêt de Loches and then, on the left, La Chartreuse du Liget. This monastery was founded by Henry II of England after the murder of Thomas à Becket. It is best-known now for its monumental entrance gate, dating from the eighteenth century, and the nearby round Chapel of St John, dating from the twelfth century, which contains some frescoes from the Romanesque period.

Those who only made it to Montrichard for lunch can reach Loches direct, by taking the D764. This passes through pleasant, rolling countryside, before sweeping in front of the Château de Montpoupon. The large thirteenth-century towers are linked by the fifteenth-century house. The gatehouse dates from the sixteenth century. Visits are possible during the summer season and include the kitchens and stables. After Genillé the road passes through the Forêt de Loches, planted to provide wood for ships, and then to Loches.

Loches contains a whole medieval city, redolent of Loire Valley history. It is worth staying a day or two in one of the hotels and sightseeing on foot. It is also a good base from which to explore the surrounding farm country (the so-called 'Paris' mushrooms are grown in caves in the vicinity). Loches has a watersports centre with a heated, covered swimming pool as well as an open-air one, and tennis courts. In mid-July there is a Peasant Market.

Loches — the keep

A medieval farm by the Indre

A quiet corner in Loches

Château de Montpoupon

It is possible to ride and walk along the many tracks in the Forêt de Loches. Cycling and fishing are among other outdoor activities available. Between 1 July and 15 September medieval Loches is floodlit at night. By day, English-speaking guides are available.

Loches was a royal château; Charles VII installed his mistress, Agnès Sorel, in it. There was nothing remarkable about a French king taking a mistress, save that Charles VII did so openly, scandalising public opinion and risking the displeasure of the Church. Agnès has always been singled out for special comment, for she is said to have been the kindest, most gentle royal mistress. The recumbent stone tomb in the château suggests these qualities as well as an innocence in her character. What makes her even more interesting is that she was painted by her friend and servant Jean Fouqet of Tours (1420-80), probably the greatest of any native Loire Valley painters. In what is known as the Melun Diptych (which is hanging in Antwerp) Fouquet paints her as the Holy Mother in his *Virgin and Child* of 1450, the year of Agnès' death.

It is possible to walk round the exterior of the medieval Cité's ramparts, which takes about 1 hour. An exploration of the old quarter also makes a pleasant stroll. A combined ticket allows entry to both the château, at one end of the Cité, and the castle keep at the other. A visit to the keep also includes the dungeons. Between the keep and the château is the church, close to which are two museums. One of these, the Musée du Terroir, is actually in the massive Porte Royale gateway.

Tours can be reached directly from Loches on the N143, a distance of about 40km (25 miles). For those spending some time in Loches, the drive up the Indre Valley is well-worthwhile. Cross the River Indre, and turn left along the far bank of the river on the D25. Recross the river to come into Chambourg. Keep to the quiet lanes by taking the D17, which follows the river. At Azay-sur-Indre is Manoir de la Follaine (this is not open) which once belonged to the Marquis de la Fayette, much honoured by Americans for his active support in their War of Independence.

There is now a pretty run along the Indre to **Cormery**. This is one of the many fortified villages to have been repeatedly pillaged and ransacked by English and French soldiers. Cormery sits pleasantly on the south bank of the Indre, adorned by an old mill and weeping willows. On the opposite bank is **Truyes** with a Romanesque church whose belfry is in five stages. Although almost nothing remains of Cormery's abbey, it is evocative of an older and more peaceful Anglo-French association. Founded in 791, the Benedictine abbey flourished for exactly 1,000 years, the Revolutionary government then sold it off for it to be virtually destroyed. Albinus lived and taught at the abbey. He was better known as Alcuin and had been a pupil at the Cloister School in York. Brought to Cormery in 796 by Charlemagne after having taught the Emperor's children and family at Aix-la-Chapelle, Alcuin of York spent 8 years spreading his love of learning. He died at Cormery in 804 but his civilising influence was exerted long after his death.

What is left of the abbey is to be found in Rue de l'Abbaye, next to the Mairie on the N143. The massive eleventh-century belfry-tower arches over the road; the brickwork is in a lozenge and scallop formation, with Romanesque bas-reliefs. A priory lodge, spiral staircase, and arches of the thirteenth-century refectory are other remnants.

Also in Cormery is the twelfth-century Church of Notre Dame-du-Fougeray with a single nave and a central cupola. Four twelfth-century statues stand in apsidal niches; a cylindrical baptismal font decorated with masks is of the same period; the frescoes came a century later. In the cemetery facing the church is yet another twelfth-century religious building, a *Lanterne des Morts* (Lantern of the Dead). These are rare in this part of France but more widespread in northern Aquitaine. The body awaiting burial was placed in the Lantern of the Dead, while higher up the tower a lamp would be lit in a small window.

After Cormery the influence of Tours is once again much in evidence, but before returning to the city, continue along the Indre a little further (keep to the D17) as far as **Montbazon**.

The town may be famous for a Foulques Nerra fortress, but it has been made to look a little ludicrous by a nineteenth-century bronze statue of the Virgin on top of what remains of the keep. You are aware of the proximity of Tours, of the N10 (the Poitiers road), and of the A10 Aquitaine autoroute.

The main N10 provides an easy run back into Tours.

6
FROM TOURS TO CHINON

The distance from Tours to Chinon is about 50km (30 miles); less than 1 hour's driving. However, a week would hardly cover all there is to see. Leave Tours by crossing the Loire northwards, although this appears to be taking you in the wrong direction. Turn left immediately onto the N152 alongside the river. **Luynes**, 8km (5 miles) downstream and just off the main road, is an engaging small town on account of its sixteenth-century houses and massive fifteenth-century oak-timbered covered market. A walk through vineyards by the D49 gives a view of the thirteenth-century château. North of Luynes, a lane climbs for 2km (1 mile) into open farmland on a plateau. On the right is a long, silent row of brick supports and six arches which carried the Roman aqueduct into Tours.

Return to Luynes and continue along the lane which joins the N152 at Pont-de-Bresme. After about 3km (2 miles) turn right where a sign says 'Monument Historique'. It leads to something of a conundrum at **Cinq-Mars-la-Pile**. A forbidding and ancient, square brick block, 30m (98ft) tall, stands on high ground. There is neither inscription nor decoration and it is solid inside. Most authorities believe it to be Gallo-Roman; others argue that it was erected by slave labour (to account for its crude brickwork) when the Alans invaded the region in AD439. No-one knows what La Pile was built for. The château at Cinq-Mars-la-Pile now consists of only two round eleventh- and twelfth-century towers whose vaulted chambers can be visited. From the top there are extensive views of the river. The gardens are a compromise between formal French layout and the English liking for natural beauty.

After Cinq-Mars comes **Langeais**, famous for its melons as well as its château. This approach is certainly the best as the castle gateway,

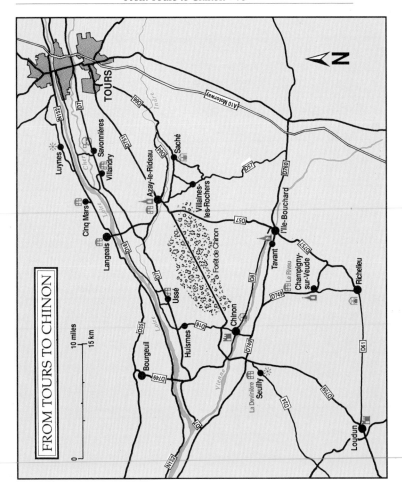

FROM TOURS TO CHINON

with its drawbridge, stands menacingly at the end of the high street. The narrow streets make parking difficult: turn right in front of the castle, then immediately left — there is a small car park on the right after about 200m (220yd).

At first sight, Langeais seems like a late medieval fortress, with solid walls and round towers. However, after walking through the gateway, the visitor sees a façade of windows dating from the early Renaissance. What is even more surprising is the fact that the whole château was built in one go, over a 4 year period from 1465, and has not been altered since. The original castle keep stands on a piece of slightly higher ground within the castle. This was built by Foulques Nerra in the tenth century and is generally accepted as the oldest keep still standing in France. The present château was built by Louis XI as protection against a Breton invasion. Less than 30 years later the threat was removed, ironically within the walls of Langeais itself, by the marriage of Charles VIII to Anne of Brittany.

The interior of the château is particularly well-furnished with period items, carefully accumulated by the previous owner, Jacques Siegfried. Most notable is the fine collection of tapestries by Flemish and Aubusson schools. As a result of this, the apartments have a 'lived-in' feel. A guided tour visits the various apartments and ends with a walk along the guards' walkway at the top of the château. One of the rooms contains a waxwork representation of the marriage of Charles VIII and Anne of Brittany.

Cross the Loire at Langeais — the only crossing point between Tours and Chinon — and at Lignières turn left on to the D7 to **Villandry**. The château at Villandry is just after the village, and there are parking spaces under the trees on either side of the road.

 The château itself, the last to be built on the banks of the Loire, is late Renaissance of 1532. It houses Spanish and Italian paintings: Velasquez, Zurbaran, Goya, Titian and Tintoretto are all represented, but the authenticity of some is questionable. Villandry's gardens make the place unique. Sixteenth-century designs for a formal French garden have been carefully reproduced. Here it is in three tiers: at the lowest level is the kitchen garden, or *jardin potager*, where sixteenth-century vegetables and herbs are grown (no potatoes; they had not yet reached France); above that the ornamental garden; uppermost the water-garden and ornamental lake. From this vantage point there are views across the Cher and the Loire.

To the side of the château are some shady terraces which allow the visitor to appreciate the layout of the gardens from a higher viewpoint. Gardeners will be fascinated by the various plants and techniques. During the summer months a craft fair is regularly held in the stable block on the opposite side of the courtyard to the château.

Slightly further up the road, at **Savonnières**, are the Caves Gouttières or Grottes Pétrifiantes, quarries exploited between the twelfth and fourteenth centuries for the Savonnières tufa, easily worked and of a particularly intense white. Countless churches and cathedrals were built with this tufa. Forgotten for 600 years, the *grottes* have calcified into stalactites and other extraordinary concretions. Objects vitrified in the caves can be bought there. The visit lasts about three-quarters of an hour (a glass of wine is included in the charge) and the cave temperature is a steady 14°C (57°F), so warm clothing is recommended. During speleological investigations of the connecting galleries, a Gallo-Roman cemetery was discovered, as was a tunnel to the garden of the château at Villandry.

Return back through Villandry but, at Le Moulinet, turn right onto the D16 which runs along the embankment at the edge of the Loire. There are plenty of picnic spots here, although parents should keep a close eye on their children as the river is deep and fast-flowing in places. The embankment, or *levée*, road (the D16) passes the bridge to Langeais, and continues for another 11km (7 miles) to Ile St Martin. By turning left here to Ussé, you will reach the **Château d'Ussé**. The best views are from the little bridge just before the T-junction in front of the castle.

There is ample parking opposite the château entrance, as well as a shady café for refreshment. Ussé is a wholly romantic fifteenth-century castle, its white walls and turrets rising out of charming terraced gardens like the backcloth to an operetta, especially when seen from the Loire *levée*. Parts of the interior can be viewed, as well as the isolated chapel in the grounds. The interior decoration of the château is lavish, especially when compared with many others elsewhere.

The D7 that runs in front of the château offers two routes to Chinon; through Huismes (via the D16) where the surrealist painter Max Ernst lived from 1954 until his death in 1976; or to the D749 alongside the Avoine nuclear power station. Either way brings the visitor to the foot of the great castle at **Chinon**.

The castle ruins are, in fact, best appreciated from the bridge, or from the opposite bank. Chinon is both a good stopping place, and a touring base; there is a good range of hotels and restaurants from which to choose. There is good self-catering accommodation in the locality too. The town and surrounding countryside are intimately linked with English history as the Plantagenets came from this area. To Henry II (of England) it was the centre of his realms, realms that stretched from the Pyrénées to the Scottish borders. He died at Chinon in 1189 and was succeeded by his son, Richard Coeur-de-Lion. Henry, Eleanor of Aquitaine, and Richard are all buried nearby at Fontevraud Abbey. Joan of Arc also came to Chinon, in 1429, to find the Dauphin.

The old quarter of Chinon, squeezed in between the castle and the river, has been carefully restored, and is largely pedestrianised. The

Villandry: the château and gardens

Château d'Ussé

Chinon

local wine-growers assembly, the 'Entonneurs Rabelaisiens' meets in caves under the castle. There is one long street through the old quarter, Rue Voltaire/Rue Haute St Maurice, with narrow streets and alleys running off it. An interesting wine museum, which uses animated figures to tell the story of wine-making, is situated just off Rue Voltaire, in Rue du Dr Gendron. A little further along Rue Voltaire is the Tourist Office. After this come several medieval houses, one of which houses a museum about Chinon, and there is also boating on the Rivers Vienne and Loire.

 The castle itself is reached either by the main road, which sweeps around the bluff on which the castle stands, or by narrow alleys of steps from the town square. Little more than the ruins of the castle remains, although it is not difficult to imagine how impressive it must have been when fully operational in the Middle Ages. Four rooms in the Royal apartments in the Château du Milieu have been restored, and display various items about the castle (there is a guided tour, but it is available in English only). There are some superb views from the gardens in the castle.

North-east of Chinon is the large Forêt de Chinon, on the other side of which is **Azay-le-Rideau**. Just off the Tours road (the D751), about 20km (12 miles) from Chinon, Azay is home to one of the prettiest Loire châteaux — certainly a contrast to Chinon. For beauty it bears comparison with Chenonceau. Of all châteaux, Balzac liked Azay best. Its name is said to derive from a *seigneur*, Rideau or Ridel d'Azay. It could also have been handed down as a reference to the curtain wall or *rideau* of the castle which stood here previously. Once it was called Azay-le-Brûlé (Azay-the-Burned) when the earlier fortress, held by the Burgundians, was burned to the ground and the prisoners killed on the order of Charles. Aged 15, he was to become Joan's 'gentle Dauphin'.

Screened by trees, Azay, like Chenonceau, is a building of grace and elegance, its white stone edifice almost seems to float on the river. In fact, it is partly built on piles sunk into the Indre's bed. Azay was created by a financier in the service of the king (Gilles Berthelot of Tours). It took 11 years to construct, between 1518 and 1529. He fell foul of the king and was forced to flee, and François I confiscated the château. A string of owners, forgotten by history, occupied Azay until the French state bought it in 1905. Inside, the building is arranged as a Renaissance museum with period furnishings, tapestries and paintings. Unlike its privately-owned counterparts, Azay's interior has a rather shabby air about it, and is something of an anti-climax compared to the exterior. During the summer months a splendid *son-et-lumière* takes place in and around the château grounds.

Do not leave the village without having walked around and visited the cool interior of St Symphorien's Church, parts of which date from the eleventh century. Leave Azay by the bridges, and turn left on to the D17, then right on to the D57 to **Villaines-les-Rochers**. Villaines is home to a wickerwork co-operative begun in 1849.

Today, eighty families, many of them living in troglodyte houses in the village, contribute their extraordinarily varied wickerwork to the modern co-operative building. You can wander round the spacious display hall and observe that the objects for sale are useful as well as decorative. You can also see demonstrations of wickerwork techniques. Special varieties of *Salix* osier shrubs are cultivated in the valleys of the Indre and Villaines. *La vannerie* is a traditional craft, handed down over the centuries within certain families. In his *Lys dans la Vallée*, Balzac refers to the basket-weavers of Villaines-les Rochers.

Make your way back to the Indre at **Saché** by taking the D27 and then turning right onto the D17. What you are likely to be confronted with before all else in this delightful village is a large, incongruous abstract work in the square. The American artist Alexander Calder (1898-1976) lived at Saché for part of his life and gave this object — a long metal arm on a pedestal, balancing a painted disc at each end — to the village. The square is large enough not to be completely dominated by the stabile.

What is called the Château de Saché is actually a simple sixteenth-to seventeenth-century *gentilhommière* or manor house. It is of no great merit in itself, and is visited because of the Balzac Museum it contains. Between 1829 and 1837 Balzac worked here a great deal through the generous hospitality of friends who owned it. It was his favourite retreat, and Saché strongly influenced his writing. *Le Père Goriot, Le Lys dans la Vallée,* and *César Birotteau* were all written here. The Balzac Museum is now a literary shrine; rooms have been left more or less as they were in his time. There are manuscripts and corrected proofs so minutely annotated in his own hand that the compositors would not work on them for more than 2 hours a day; anything more brought on eye-strain and headaches. There are figurines of the characters in his *Comédie Humaine*, that enormous portrait of a whole society in ferment and abandoning itself to greed and vice, created by a writer who powerfully and prolifically breathed life into the phantoms of his literary creation. A *son-et-lumière* about Balzac and Saché is performed during the summer

The Cardinal's statue, Richelieu

← *Azay-le-Rideau*

months. From Saché return to Chinon through Azay.

For a leisurely drive parallel to the Vienne, leave Chinon by the D8. At various places it is possible to get down to the clear and tranquil river's edge. Turn left where a signpost points across the vineyards to Cravant-les-Côteaux. Just beyond is **Vieux Bourg**, the nave of whose church (there is a small museum inside) is a rare example of early tenth-century Carolingian architecture. Return to the D8 and cross the river at l'Ile-Bouchard. To see the little Romanesque Church of St Nicolas at **Tavant**, follow the D760 west for 2km (1 mile) and look out for a sharp and narrow entrance to the lane which leads to the church. It holds twelfth-century frescoes of an originality almost unique in France.

An interesting excursion at the weekend can be made possible by abandoning the car, and taking a steam train through the country-side from Chinon to Richelieu. Alternatively, you can take the car and stop on the way at Le Rivau, just off the D749. This delightful fortified manor house (see the sign on the gate for entry arrange-ments) is set in pleasant gardens, and is reached by a drawbridge. Owned by an artist, the interior has been carefully restored and is well-furnished. The prison and the iron masks are fascinating. A couple of rooms contain works by the artist-owner, who still lives in the house.

Continue towards Richelieu, pausing at **Champigny-sur-Veude** to view the lovely Renaissance chapel, almost all that is left of a now vanished château. The outstanding stained glass forms a complete set, probably the work of the master glass-makers of the Bourbon-nais. Another $6^{1}/_{2}$km (4 miles) further on is **Richelieu** itself.

The town is named after Richelieu, the Great Cardinal. In 1624 the Cardinal became the King's chief Minister; the following year work began here on the construction of a château, and a complete planned town. At the time, it was looked upon as a perfect example of town planning. It is laid out in a rectangle, 700m by 500m (763yd by 545yd), with three principal entrances. The gatehouses still stand. The Grande Rue runs from north to south, lined by twenty-eight identi-cal, handsome houses. In the Place du Marché there is a splendidly raftered, covered market. The Hôtel de Ville contains a small mu-seum. Of Cardinal Richelieu's château, little remains other than the impressive park.

From Richelieu head back to Chinon by taking the D61 across country to **Loudun**. The narrow streets of this pretty little town wind around the remains of the eleventh-century tower, which was built by Foulques Nerra. There are some fine views from the top. At

Loudun take the D759 back towards Chinon. Do take time, however, to turn off this road onto the D24 to visit **Seuilly**. This small village, overlooked by the Château de Coudray-Montpensier (this is not open), has an interesting street of troglodyte houses. To find them, turn right after the Mairie and then left again. These houses and small farms are actually cut into the hill behind, so that part of the building is underground — occasionally there is the surprising sight of chimneys protruding from what appears to be a field or an orchard.

Seuilly is also where La Devinière is situated (this is well-signposted). It was here that François Rabelais — writer, physician and scholar — spent his childhood. La Devinière, the simple country house of his lawyer father, is now a little museum. Much of his ribald youthful fantasy spilled into his *Gargantua* (1534) in which all the place names of the district occur.

It is only a short distance from Seuilly back to Chinon.

*Dovecote at
La Devinière*

La Devinière

l'Ile-Bouchard Town Hall

The Romanesque Church of St Nicholas at Tavant

7
FROM CHINON TO ANGERS

T he confluence of the Vienne (this flows through Chinon) and the Loire marks another change in direction for the latter, as it swings north-west towards Angers. It also marked the meeting point of Anjou, Touraine and Poitou. Links with the English monarchy abound, especially the Plantagenets, and there are no stronger links than at **Fontevraud Abbey**, just downstream from Chinon.

Founded in the eleventh century, the monastery soon comprised five separate buildings: for monks, nuns, repentant women, lepers and other sick persons. In its heyday, it housed 5,000 people, always under the authority of an abbess, who was usually an aristocrat.

Fontevraud found favour with the Plantagenets while they were Counts of Anjou, and they heaped wealth onto the abbey. Henry, Count of Anjou and Duke of Normandy, brought his wife Eleanor of Aquitaine to Fontevraud. Eleanor was the divorced wife of the French King, and she had brought as her dowry Poitou, the Saintonge, Limousin, and Gascony — in essence, the whole area from the Pyrénées to the Loire and inland to the Massif Central. When Henry became King of England, his possessions stretched across the western half of France, as well as England.

Both Henry and Eleanor were buried at Fontevraud, to be joined later by their son Richard Coeur-de-Lion. The crypt also contained the hearts of Henry's other son, John Lackland ('Bad King John'), and his son, Henry III. This last Henry was responsible for rebuilding Westminster Abbey in London, which then became the English sovereign's resting place.

The painted effigies of Henry II, Eleanor of Aquitaine and Richard I remain intact, despite the desecration wrought by Huguenots in 1562, Revolutionaries in 1793 who jumbled all the bones together, and Napoleon who turned the place into a prison in 1804, which it remained until 1963. A huge programme of restoration is now underway.

There is much to see in the church and the abbey buildings, and the guided tour is a long one. The church is huge and bears many resemblances to churches further south in Aquitaine (as a result of the Anjou/Aquitaine links). A lot of work is still going on, so there is always something to see. In the arm of the transept are the effigies of Henry, Eleanor and Richard, behind a perspex screen. The cloisters are richly decorated with carvings, and the chapterhouse contains murals. The refectory has been well-restored and often plays host to concerts. The medieval kitchens are quite astonishing for their beauty and utility. From outside, a cluster of twenty pepper-pot chimneys are connected to artfully placed flues which extracted smoke from five fireplaces inside. A number of the abbey's outbuildings often feature exhibitions and displays, as the abbey is now also an important arts centre.

Montsoreau, 5km (3 miles) away on the D947, is back on the Loire itself. An agreeable town with a sandy beach, it has a fifteenth-century château — part fortress, part country seat — with lovely views of the Loire, the Vienne and vineyards. Its Musée des Goums deals with the French conquest of Morocco. Just south of here is Moulin de la Herpinière, a fifteenth-century windmill whose grindstone was lodged underground. There is now an artists' workshop open to the public.

After Montsoreau the D947 runs alongside the Loire, through a succession of villages, most of which have wine-making as part of their economy. The south-facing fields on top of the riverside cliffs are ideal for vineyards, the caves in the white cliffs are perfect for storing wine. The D947 then reaches Saumur, passing on the left the seemingly huge Church of Notre Dame-des-Ardilliers, once a major centre of pilgrimage.

Those who prefer to be diverted by more worldly things than Plantagenet kings, may prefer to get to Saumur on the north bank of the Loire, through the Bourgeuil vineyards. Leave Chinon on the D749, go past the silver globes of the Avoine nuclear power station, and over the river. The road leads straight to **Bourgeuil**. The village has plenty of growers ready to sell their wares. The vineyards spread around the village and up the hillsides at the edge of the Loire floodplain.

Return to the river and follow the N152 along the riverbank. Not far from the bridge, by the power station, is the delightful Château

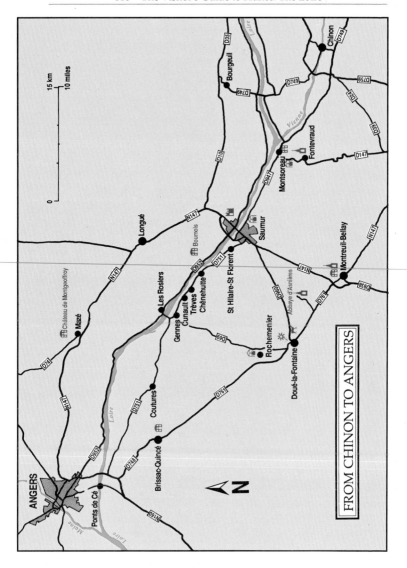

FROM CHINON TO ANGERS

The Plantagenet tombs at Fontevraud

des Réaux, where it is possible to stay and where guests are treated as one of the family. The riverside road offers views of both river and countryside, and ultimately of Saumur Castle high above the rooftops.

Saumur retains an air of old-world provincialism. When it was a Protestant stronghold its population was larger than today's until the Revocation of the Edict of Nantes in 1685 when thousands fled the town. Atmosphere, history, food and wine make Saumur (literally translated as 'safe wall') appealing to the visitor. Buildings constructed out of the local white tufa rock catch the eye, as do the Angers roof-slates. Saumur's strategic position has ensured a political and commercial importance greater than its actual size.

Most of the town lies south of the Loire. On the elongated island — once known as l'Ile d'Or — fishermen lived in almost total autonomy in King René's time. There is parking along the quays (where weekend market stalls add vitality to the scene), near the château and elsewhere in the town centre. Hotels and restaurants are modestly priced.

Tufa becomes whiter with age, and so the old château looks like a white icing-sugar fortress. The best first impressions are those from across the river; you see the château high on its *butte* (once lined with windmills) over the town. Four-sided but irregularly shaped, it is supported by four machicolated, pepper-pot towers. From the battlements the Loire can be seen spreading far on either side. Inside are two outstanding, specialist museums. One is the Museum of Decorative Arts displaying highest quality china from many parts of Europe, as well as paintings, tapestries, furniture and carved wooden statuettes. The other, the Horse Museum, traces the history of the horse from the earliest times and has a display of riding tackle from around the world.

A guided tour (this is available in English) takes visitors around the castle, although afterwards one is at liberty to wander around the lawned terraces overlooking the town. The castle has ample car parking for those who cannot face the stiff, uphill walk from the town centre. Saumur offers a good selection of shops and cafés, and the twisting streets below the château have one or two interesting buildings.

Saumur is also home to the French Cavalry. At the opposite end of the town to the château (about 15 minutes walk along Rue Beaupaire) is the Cavalry School and Museum. The famous Cadre Noir is attached to the Ecole Nationale d'Equitation (National Riding School), at St Hilaire-St Florent, just outside Saumur itself. St Hilaire-St Florent is also where Saumur's sparkling wine is made.

A long street of *salons de dégustation* allows you to taste and buy. Look out for Appellation Crémant de Loire, which is probably the best. Chalk cliffs are also exploited for mushroom growing, and the fascinating Musée du Champignon shows how different varieties of commercial mushrooms are grown.

A short distance south-west of Saumur on the D960 is **Doué-la-Fontaine** which is a mixture of broad, modern streets and an old town built on the pitted chalk plateau. Below ground there are caves, some of which are still used for storage, but most have been abandoned. Doué is best known for its nurseries and rose-gardens. The Jardin des Roses is on Route de Soulanger. In mid-July the annual Rose Festival (Journées des Roses) is held in the open quarries which the Romans may have worked in the suburb of Douce. The arena is used for theatre and music shows. Underneath this there are cavernous vaults where whole communities once lived. Another attraction is the Parc Zoologique des Minières, on Route de Cholet. A variety of mammals and birds live in 10 acres of land formerly taken up by quarries.

At the village of **Rochemenier** (off the D69 and west along the

D177 for 1km ($^1/_2$ mile) is a remarkable underground Peasant Museum. Until the 1930s, the whole village occupied chalk caves (*caves demeurantes*), and the museum, consisting of two previous farms, shows how troglodytic peasants lived and worked. A similar subterranean museum is at La Fosse (take the D177 to the east towards Forges for 5km (3 miles), then right). However, this one is occupied by a family and animals; a living example of an unusual, bygone way of life.

The D761 goes straight to Montreuil-Bellay on the banks of the Thouet. Halfway along the road, a short detour to the left brings you to the ruins of Abbaye d'Asnières whose chancel is a lovely example of Angevin Gothic. There are also some charming fourteenth-century stone carvings in the abbot's chapel and oratory.

Montreuil-Bellay is in a most picturesque setting: there are gardens by the river dotted with islets and spanned by a bridge, an old water-mill, a ruined twelfth-century church, the castle, a fifteenth-century church, sections of medieval walls and two gatehouses. The present château, built in the fifteenth century, had cannonballs rather than archers in mind. The thirteen flanking towers had flat roofs from which artillery could be fired. Visitors are shown the medieval kitchens, wine-press, bathrooms, circular stairways leading to four suites in the Petit-Château, and the seigneurial chapel, (this is much restored), within the castle walls.

Another splendid example of Angevin Gothic architecture is at Le Puy-Notre-Dame on a high mound 8km (5 miles) west of Montreuil-Bellay. A treasure of the church is the jewelled Girdle of Our Lady brought from Jerusalem. Return to Saumur from Montreuil by the N147.

Those travelling from Saumur to Angers are offered a wide choice of routes. Head south-west to Doué-la-Fontaine, then up the D761 through **Brissac-Quincé** — pausing, perhaps, to look at the château which has a late sixteenth-century façade.

Crossing the river to the far bank gives you two options — follow the D952 along the river bank, or head inland to follow the N147. On the former, make a diversion after leaving Saumur to visit Boumois, a pretty fifteenth-century château with a fine collection of weapons. On the latter, turn off at Mazé to visit Château de Montgeoffroy, an elegant eighteenth-century château which has remained in the same family since it was built. As a result, furniture and furnishings have been kept together and preserved.

The nicest route, however, is to leave Saumur through St Hilaire-St Florent. The road, the D751, runs between cliff and river and is

Saumur: the castle and site on the River Loire

Troglodyte home near Doué-la-Fontaine

very pretty in places. **Chênehutte-les-Tuffeaux** holds an annual mushroom fair in May. Continue along the D751 to **Trèves**. Trèves (translated as 'Truce', a name invented with sardonic humour by Foulques Nerra for his castle here) is a tiny village with a squat Romanesque church cowering beneath a round, fifteenth-century keep.

Next is **Cunault**, another tiny village, but one with a large Romanesque church. The exterior hides a fascinating interior, with superbly carved capitals, and both wall and roof paintings. After Gennes, the road sweeps inland to join up with the D952 into Angers.

8
ANGERS, NORTHERN ANJOU AND ANCENIS

W ith a population of over 140,000, **Angers** is the largest city in the region (although the conurbation of Tours makes that city considerably larger). Most of the interesting places are compressed within the old town of Angers which is bounded by broad, tree-lined boulevards. The bigger section of Old Angers is behind the east bank of the River Maine where the castle and cathedral are situated. Two bridges take the boulevards across the river.

Angers makes a good headquarters for leisurely sightseeing on foot as there are numerous hotels within or just outside these boulevards. Motorists who prefer to stay in the countryside yet within easy reach of Angers will find agreeable hotels at Cheffes, Matheflon, Les Rosiers, Gennes, Chavagnes, Brissac-Quincé, Rochefort-sur-Loire and Le Lion d'Angers. All of these are in a radius of 30km (20 miles) from Angers. In the city itself, metered parking places are available quite close to the chief sights.

 Upon entering Angers, the visitor will identify the château as the dominating landmark and it is the first place to make for. Its presence is imperious and it commands attention by the sheer weight and power of its seventeen bastion towers. These are 40m to 50m (130ft to 160ft) high (once they were taller and capped by pepperpot roofs), linked by a double row of walls which are roughly pentagonal in shape. The curtain wall is more than 1km ($^1/_2$ mile) long. Gardens are planted out between inner and outer walls.

The seventeen bastion towers splay outwards like gigantic elephants feet, as though to grip the dark grey metamorphosed rock on which the castle was built. The towers are dark shale, their glowering monotony relieved by bands of white limestone. Much of Angers was built with this shale, and drew upon itself the epithet 'Black Angers'. The blue-grey slate of Angers has roofed countless châteaux and mansions. Indeed, Angers represents a marked change, for the tufa stone of the châteaux higher up the river has suddenly given way to this dark, forbidding shale.

Part of the feudal castle still has a deep, broad dry moat where a herd of fallow deer lives. Enter the castle by the drawbridge over the moat from the Promenade du Bout du Monde. Splendidly sited for its strategic needs in medieval times, its bastions protected the castle on the three sides away from the river. Its western flank was then washed by the Maine. Beyond the far side lay the hostile lands of the Dukes of Brittany, allies of the English.

In the third century AD a continuous protective wall, more than 1km ($^1/_2$ mile) long, was built to hold back barbarian invasions. Fragments of it are lodged in the south wall of the cathedral's sacristy.

A wooden fortress erected by Foulques Nerra had stood on the site before St Louis (Louis IX of the Capetian dynasty) rebuilt it in stone between 1220 and 1240. Over the centuries, parts of the castle's interior have been demolished and rebuilt. The surviving wing of the fifteenth-century Logis Royal, the king's quarters put up by Louis II of Anjou, stands next to the chapel. His wife, Yolande of Aragon, had the latter constructed of white tufa stone. Inside the chapel, note the vaulting and the carved keystones which include a reproduction of the True Cross of Baugé.

In the Logis Royal are four fifteenth-century Flemish tapestries of the Passion. Perhaps the most delightful is *La Dame à l'Orgue* which depicts a woman playing a portable organ, accompanied by other elegant characters.

More tapestries are exhibited in the Logis du Gouverneur, built in the eighteenth century, across the courtyard. These fifteenth- to eighteenth-century works are only modest introductions to the real masterpiece of the Château d'Angers, the tapestries or *tentures* of *The Apocalypse*. A special building, the Grande Galerie, houses the 100m (330ft) long and 5m (16ft) high tapestries. Once they were more than half as long again. A red velvet background throws into relief the figures conveying the passion and pathos inherent in the theme of sin and damnation which so absorbed the medieval mind.

Commissioned by Louis I of Anjou in 1373, the tapestry was made in the Paris workshops of Nicolas Bataille between 1377 and 1380 from designs by Hennequin de Bruges which are in the Bibliothèque

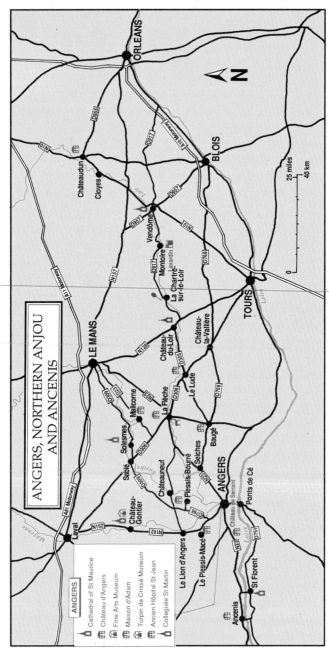

ANGERS, NORTHERN ANJOU AND ANCENIS

ANGERS

🛡 Cathedral of St Maurice
🏰 Château d'Angers
🏛 Fine Arts Museum
🏛 Maison d'Adam
🏛 Turpin de Crissé Museum
🏛 Ancien Hôpital St Jean
🏛 Collegiale St Martin

Château d'Angers →

Nationale in Paris. Seventy-seven pieces survive; faded but majestic and poignant, a remarkable achievement of preservation when one considers their history. The pieces were transported in 1400 to Arles in Provence for the wedding of Louis II to Yolande. Stored at Baugé in 1476 for 4 years, then bundled away in Angers Cathedral for 300 years, they were displayed once a year.

In 1782 the church tried to sell *The Apocalypse* but no-one offered to buy it. During the Revolution the tapestries were thrown into the streets. People helped themselves, and pieces did every conceivable duty, from being used as horse-blankets to draught-stoppers. In 1843 the Bishop of Angers bought up, for 300 francs, all the remains he could trace (mostly off a rubbish dump). The maltreated tapestries were once again displayed only on feast days, they left the cathedral for their present home in 1952.

There is a portable audio guide commentary in English, or you can follow the explanations of each scene in the windows. Some critics have said that, marvellous though they are, the tapestries have lost some of their mysterious magnetism since coming to the Grande Galerie. For most visitors, however, the exhibition is clear and enlightening.

The tapestries of Angers are by no means exhausted; the city is a major centre of tapestries that can be seen by the public. Across the river is La Doutre (*d'outre* meaning 'beyond' and implying, many years ago, a socially inferior status). This is reached by the upstream bridge of Pont de la Haute Chaine.

 Ten tapestries are displayed in what was once the huge ward in the former Hospital of St John (Ancien Hôpital St Jean). They belong to an entirely different epoch from those of the *Apocalypse*, though they were inspired by Bataille's work. These ten panels, 80m (260ft) long, were begun in 1957 by Jean Lurçat and completed in 1966. The collection is called *Le Chant du Monde* (The Song of the World). Lurçat, a humanist of our time, has used abstract symbols, riotous colours and patterns against a sombre black background to express his fears of the genocidal instinct in today's techno-civilisation. He makes this clear in the titles he gives to the first four panels: 'The Great Menace', 'The Man of Hiroshima', 'The Great Charnel House', 'The End of Everything'. Later, he comes to more optimistic themes.

The series is acknowledged as a great work of art and was created by a man who revived the impetus of tapestry-making. Whether the moral messages and sentiments are anything more than muddy and confused will depend on the viewer's intuitive perceptions and identification with the humanistic philosophy of Lurçat's old age.

Whatever response the visitor has to the tapestries, the old hospital itself is well-worth looking over. It was founded in 1174 by Henry II as part of his penance for the assassination of Archbishop Becket of Canterbury. The medieval hospital ward where the Lurçats are situated is huge, spacious and beautifully vaulted. At one end of it is all the attractive paraphernalia of a seventeenth-century pharmacy. In the hospital gardens are a few remnants of Angers' Gallo-Roman past, and behind the chapel there is a wine museum.

This visit across the river is something of a digression. Although there are some other old buildings in La Doutre, the main sightseeing is confined to the east bank of the Maine. The Cathedral of St Maurice is best approached by the rising steps of the Montée St Maurice which leads to the west front. A late Romanesque façade is surmounted by two dissimilar towers separated by a third, put up in the sixteenth century. The tympanum is filled by Christ seated in majesty with four Evangelists.

The cathedral was roofed in an interesting way. An earlier church on the site had burned down but its outer walls were intact, and it was decided to use them to construct an exceptionally wide nave. The architect dealt with the problem of the stress such a roof-span entailed by raising the keystone of the ogival arches 3m (10ft) higher than those of the side and cross arches. This high pitch of the groin-vaulting was the first to be used, and so became known as Angevin vaulting, which prepared the way for the Gothic style.

It took 80 years to build St Maurice. By the time they came to tackle the transept and choir, enough experience and confidence had been gained for the builders to make the vaulting lighter and more elegant through the use of additional ribs to strengthen the arches.

More tapestries — from Aubusson — hang in the cathedral, but they are not easy to see. The stained-glass windows start from the twelfth century, and there are also modern ones. The Treasury contains some interesting pieces: there is a Roman font used for baptising the Dukes of Anjou and a red porphyry urn which had belonged to King René.

A little to the south of the cathedral is the Logis Barrault, facing the Jardin des Beaux-Arts. In this impressive fifteenth-century Renaissance building is the Fine Arts Museum (Musée des Beaux-Arts). As far as local art is concerned, the main attraction is a collection of plaster casts by the sculptor and medallionist, David d'Angers (1788-1856), son of a woodcarver of Angers. The house where he was born, 38 Rue David d'Angers, is marked with a plaque. Near the château is a statue of King René by him, and a marble statue of Ste Cécile

Market day in Angers

behind the high altar of the cathedral.

In the museum are statues and busts of many famous people of his day — Paganini, Goethe, Victor Hugo and Balzac being among them. The fact that this is a good provincial museum is underlined by the diversity of paintings from various schools; Fragonard, Watteau,

Angers: the Old Town →

Boucher, Corot, Chardin, Mignard, Van Loo, Greuze and Ingres, to mention only some representatives of the French School.

Just west of Logis Barrault, in a garden, are the romantic ruins of Chapelle Toussaint. This was accidentally blown up in 1815 when the place was being used as a military arsenal. In the opposite direction, east of the Logis, is a thick-walled square keep, Tour St Aubin. This had been both bell-tower and place of refuge for the monks of the twelfth-century Abbaye St Aubin which lay at a little distance from the tower.

Rebuilt in the seventeenth century, the abbey is now part of the Préfecture. During office hours, it is possible to see the remarkable carved rounded arcades of a Romanesque cloister and chapterhouse doorway which came to light in 1836. Best-preserved of these stone carvings are those depicting David and Goliath, the latter being felled wearing a coat of Norman armour. In another scene, his head is presented to Saul. Below these, thirteenth-century frescoes, which are in a fine state of preservation, tell the story of the Magi.

Still in the Old Town is Hôtel Pincé, just beyond Place du Ralliement. A graceful Renaissance building, it houses the Turpin de Crissé Museum. This has Greek and Etruscan vases, *objets d'art* from China and Japan, sixteenth-century painted enamels, and engravings depicting the history of fashion in France.

Behind the Post Office is the Collégiale St Martin. Built on the site of an early Christian cemetery, which can be seen with its sarcophagi in the crypt, the collegiate church is something of a rarity for it is a largely intact, ninth-century Carolingian building. It was founded by Foulques Nerra in one of his occasional moods of repentance and benevolence.

Here and there, when you are strolling about the narrow streets or *ruelles* of the old quarters, delightful examples of fifteenth- to eighteenth-century merchants' houses can be found. One of these is the Maison d'Adam, Place Ste Croix; a fifteenth-century half-timbered house with five overhanging storeys and diamond-shaped lattices over the façades. Its timbers are covered with secular carvings. Hôtel du Croissant, in Rue St Aignan, is also worth seeing.

Angers, strictly speaking, is not on the Loire itself, although it is a Loire Valley city in both style and history. However, it is very much a city of rivers. The Maine runs below the château walls and, immediately upstream, the Mayenne, the Sarthe, and the Loir all join and empty into the Maine which, in turn, joins the River Loire just below Angers.

These three rivers all make pleasing excursions from Angers, with plenty of historical and general interest alike for the Loire Valley visitor. Boats can be hired on all the rivers and offer a very different holiday experience, one based on exploring the countryside.

The Mayenne winds its way northwards towards Normandy. Both the main N162 road and the much less crowded riverside lanes offer a great deal. Just off the N162 (and well-signposted) is the **Château de Plessis-Macé**. In the twelfth century it was a fortress against hostile Brittany, its fifteenth-century buildings are much restored in a flamboyant Gothic style. The spacious interior is furnished.

Le Lion d'Angers (not connected with a lion but from the Latin *legio*, indicating a military base) is a little west of the N162 and lies on the River Oudon. Just outside is the national stud and racecourse at Château l'Isle-Briand. Visits are possible by advance arrangement.

From Le Lion d'Angers the N162 heads for Château-Gontier in a dead straight line. There are several minor châteaux which are just a short distance off the main road.

Le Bois-Mauboucher, south-west of Chambellay, stands by a large lake. Dating from the fifteenth and seventeenth centuries, it has been restored and furnished — it also has a picture gallery. **Percher**, north of Le Lion d'Angers on the N162, is in mixed Gothic and Renaissance styles. **Magnanne**, south-west of Ménil, is in the formal style of Louis XIV, built of brick, and has fine interior woodwork, furniture and paintings. **St Ouen** at Chemazé is an early sixteenth-century building of white tufa. It is richly decorated and there is also a simple chapel and house.

Château-Gontier is an important cattle-market divided by the Mayenne. Narrow, irregular streets and riverside quays make the old town picturesque. In the Romanesque Church of St Jean are frescoes and there are pleasant river views from the terraces behind it. There is also a museum with paintings, sculptures and antiquities.

Cross the river, at Château-Gontier, and return to the Angers road by way of Coudray, Daon, Marigné and **Chenillé-Changé**. This pretty riverside village has an attractive watermill which looks rather like a castle. The countryside around this area was home to a major Royalist uprising in 1793. It was called the 'Chouannerie', after the call signs the rebels made — that of an owl hoot (a tawny owl is a *chathuant* in French). Small groups fought a guerilla war amongst the hedges and lanes. The uprising was quickly put down, and thousands were shot or guillotined in the repression that followed.

The Sarthe was once the major link between Le Mans and Angers. Take the D52 from Angers towards Châteauneuf-sur-Sarthe. At

The impressive carved entrance to Angers Cathedral

A modern fountain in Angers

Tiercé turn left onto the D74 to the Château du Plessis-Bourré. This typical fairytale castle is reflected in the moat that surrounds it. The fifteenth-century building has white walls, blue-grey slate roofs, pepperpot towers, interior courtyard and arcaded galleries. The interior is impressive too, especially the guard-room with a coffered ceiling which was painted in the fifteenth century with amusing allegorical figures.

Châteauneuf-sur-Sarthe is a busy riverside town with simple hotel accommodation, some good restaurants and a selection of shops. Continue to follow the river, the best route being the D108 to Chemiré, then, switching banks, take the D159 to **Sablé-sur-Sarthe**. Sablé has some small hotels and plenty of shops, but little character. Perhaps that impression is gained because the next place is so overwhelming. From Sablé take the short drive along the D138 to **Solesmes**. Here the attraction is the majestic and world famous Gregorian chant sung by the Benedictine monks in the abbey. Mass can be attended every morning and Vespers every evening.

Solesmes is where the art of Gregorian plainchant was rediscovered and restored. There is a shop where records and books are available. Opposite the abbey is a good hotel, the Grand. Although the abbey was founded in the eleventh century, the present buildings date from the late nineteenth century and are quite austere. For a good view of the abbey building, go past the abbey, cross the bridge and turn left into Port de Juigné. Another left turn opposite the café leads into a small square beside the river. Alternatively, after crossing the bridge, turn right and continue to Juigné-sur-Sarthe, where there is an observation point.

From Juigné take the D22, then turn right onto a small side road to Avoise. Follow the road until it meets the D309. Turn right here and cross the river into Parcé, which has some delightful old houses overlooking the water. From here, follow the D8 to **Malicorne**. On entering the village, you will see a pretty, moated château (this is not open), and then a shady car park beside a mill on the river. It is a nice place to picnic, although there are a couple of restaurants in the village; several potters work here too. From Malicorne it is a straightforward run to Le Mans, or it is possible to return to Angers by way of La Flèche and then the N23.

By the time the Loir joins the Sarthe and the Mayenne above Angers, it is a peaceful, meadow-lined river which has cut small chalk embankments. It is a more intimate, small scale version of The Loire and it, too, is now useless to commerce — pleasure boats and fishermen have the stream to themselves.

Running north-east from Angers, the N23 is the direct road to Seiches and La Flèche. A quieter way to Seiches is to leave the N23 5.5km (3$^1/_2$ miles) out of Angers for the D52. If you turn right onto the D192 at La Dionière, this road will take you to **Villevêque** where tools of 400,000 years ago have been found. Cross the Loir, turn right onto the D109 and pass a dolmen on the right, before coming to the agreeable little market-town of Seiches on the left bank. Beyond Matheflon is Château du Verger, or rather, the servants' quarters of what had once been perhaps the biggest and finest château anywhere in the valley. The reason it was pulled down by Cardinal de Rohan in the eighteenth century is a mystery. An ancestor had built it 300 years earlier to receive kings and queens in fullest splendour.

Make a little detour to the village of **Huillé**, reached by heading north to Baracé and then turning right onto the D68. This has a few delightful sixteenth- and seventeenth-century houses. From here, continue to **Durtal** on the main road. Only the courtyard of Durtal's château can be visited. Porte Véron is what is left of the eleventh-century ramparts. To the south is the extensive Forêt de Chambiers which has oaks, maritime pines, a stream, lakes and footpaths.

Traffic roars through the narrow main road of **Bazouges** but there is a free car park under the trees outside the church which is the chief reason for stopping. From the outside, thick simple walls show its twelfth-century origin. The wooden vaults inside were painted in the fifteenth century. There is a sixteenth-century château close to the Loir.

La Flèche has a population of 16,500. It makes a good excursion centre. In the late tenth century a castle was put up in the middle of the Loir. Rebuilt by the Carmelites in 1620, what is left now is part of the Hôtel de Ville. Charming river views are to be had from the middle of the bridge. Henri IV, most popular of any French king for the prosperity he strove to bring and his courageous and amiable character, decreed that a place of learning be instituted in his Château Neuf at La Flèche by the Jesuits.

The king had a strong attachment to the town. He was conceived there (although born at Pau) and spent much of his youth in Château Neuf. The college was created in 1603. In its heyday, 1,500 students worked there. Its most famous pupil was René Descartes (1596-1650) who profoundly influenced French thinking. Sweeping aside the philosophical tenets of his day, he applied a mathematical approach to every aspect of knowledge.

When the Jesuits were expelled in 1762, the college was converted to a preparatory school for the Ecole Militaire in Paris. The Revolution shut it down but in 1808 Napoleon reopened it as the Prytanée Impérial Militaire. So uncouth were the manners of its pupils that they were nicknamed 'Brutions'. *Prytanée* derives from the Greek but its meaning was distorted by the Revolution to signify an institution where officers' sons received a free education so as to enter a *Grande Ecole*. It has a similar purpose today. The entrance arch in Rue du Collège is surmounted by a bust of Henri IV; an urn in the seventeenth-century Chapelle St Louis is said to contain the ashes of his heart and those of his wife, Marie de Médici.

It is also worth taking a look at the little Romanesque Chapelle Notre Dame-des-Vertus which contains woodcarvings brought from Château du Verger outside Seiches.

One popular excursion is to the zoo at **Le Tertre-Rouge**, 5km (3 miles) south-east on the D104. In pine woods which cover 18 acres there are various mammals, ranging from monkeys to elephants; birds, especially birds of prey; reptiles and snakes in glass-sided boxes. A museum illustrates the region's wildlife with dioramas, an idea conceived by the naturalist, Jacques Bouillault.

South of La Flèche is **Baugé**, about 18km (11 miles) away on the

Château du Plessis-Bourré

D938. Now a small farming town surrounded by pleasant wood-land, it has several interesting buildings. The Town Hall is housed in what was the château; and the Hôpital St Joseph contains its original panelled pharmacy. The town's main claim to fame is housed in the Chapelle des Filles du Coeur de Marie. It is a double-armed cross, found in Constantinople in the thirteenth century, and supposedly made from pieces of the True Cross. This double-armed cross became an emblem of the Dukes of Anjou, although it is better known today as the Cross of Lorraine.

East from La Flèche there is a very pleasant drive on the D13 through Mareil-sur-Loir, past the fifteenth-century Château de Gallerande on the left, through Pringé to Luché-Pringé, and then turning right beyond the village. This little rural ride takes you through luscious riverside vegetation to Le Port-des-Roches, and the drive can be continued through the sleepy countryside.

By taking the D306 south-east from La Flèche, the visitor comes to

Solesmes Abbey

Le Lude. Le Lude puts on lavish *son-et-lumière* shows; full dramatic advantage is taken of château, river and gardens. The square château, which has a round tower at each corner, dates from various eras and is much restored. A diversity of period furnishings ornament the halls and rooms.

The D306 keeps as close as it can to the Loir. **Vaas** (*Vedacium* in Gallo-Roman days) has a well-arranged beach and a medieval castle. The latter was captured and recaptured by the French and English alike. **Château-du-Loir**'s old town clusters round Eglise St Guinga- lois. The D73B goes north to follow the pretty valley of the Yre to Beaumont-Pied-de-Boeuf and Jupilles, surrounded by the Forêt de Bercé which covers some 13,800 acres. The trees are mostly of common oak, maritime and Scots pine, Spanish chestnut, and beech. Guided tours of the Futaie des Clos start from the Chêne Boppe (this is named after a distinguished forestry expert and was blasted by lightning in 1936). Forest tracks (*routes forestières*) lead to the sources of two streams, Fontaine de la Coudre and, further east, Sources de l'Hermitière. At **Jupilles** you can visit the woodcraft museum, Musée du Bois.

South-east of the Forêt de Bercé is the riverside resort of **La Chartre-sur-le-Loir** surrounded by the Val du Loir vineyards: La Chartre, the other Vouvray, Marçon, Ruillé (Clos de Sous les Bois), Lhomme and its prestigious Clos des Janières. La Chartre is one of the Stations Vertes de Vacances whose amenities such as hotels, campsites, swimming pools and tennis courts are set in rural surroundings. Days can be spent ambling about the tranquil countryside, visiting churches, manor houses and vineyards.

At **Poncé**, the sixteenth century-château, restored some 60 years ago, stands at the foot of a chalk cliff. The tall building has a Renaissance staircase of six straight flights in parallel. They pass through coffered vaults decorated with innumerable mythological sculptures. In the formal garden is a large pigeon-loft, complete with turning ladders. A path clambers the cliff, at the top is a museum of local crafts and a studio where potters work and sell their products. At the western entrance to the village, at Moulin de Paillard by the river, are two workshops producing a wide range of artefacts. In Poncé Church are some faded murals dating from 1170-80. One is a battle scene between Saracens and Crusaders, a somewhat rare theme.

After travelling a short distance upstream, turn right to **Couture**. Just short of the village is Manoir de la Possonnière, birthplace of the 'Prince of Poets', Pierre de Ronsard (1524-85). The rambling, unpretentious Renaissance house, with Latin and French inscriptions carved in stone, cannot be visited; only the outside can be seen when the owners are absent. Some of the wine cellars were hewn out of the rock. Possonnière comes from the word *poinçon*, a liquid measure which is called a puncheon in English. It describes a cask holding between 72 and 120 gallons, and is a suitable name for the wine-loving Ronsard household.

Ronsard became leader of a group of poets called La Pléiade which aimed to enrich the French language by imitating the masterpieces of classical antiquity and writing elegant poetry for the élite of the court. In this aim he was joined by his friend Joachim du Bellay (1522-60), another Angevin poet, born at La Turmelière outside Liré and not far from Nantes.

Ronsard became a page at court, and lived in Scotland and England before returning to the court of France. Illness induced deafness, and he turned to writing the sonnets by which he is remembered. Successive kings patronised him; he was on friendly terms with Elizabeth I and Mary Queen of Scots. A prey to gout, he retired in 1572 to his priories of Ste Madeleine de Croixval (the ruins are outside Marcé) or Ste Cosme-de-Tours, where he died. The tombs of Ronsard's parents are in Couture Church, where he was baptised. A commemorative plaque has been placed on l'Isle Verte where Ronsard wished to be buried. His poems sing sensuous praises to many corners: Vendôme, Troo, Croixval, Couture, Tours, Blois, Talcy and Bourgueil.

Troo is an unusual place. It sits on top of a steep hill, its belfry visible from the valley. Its name can be written Troo or Trôo. The latter is a kind of pictorial image of the belfry roof, but Michelin leaves the circumflex off its map name. Narrow, stepped streets, bits of feudal walls and subterranean passages called *caforts* make the little place labyrinthine and old. The impression is heightened by the remains of a medieval lazar-house, the Maladrerie Ste Catherine. From La Butte, the tumulus offers a broad panorama over chimneys of cave-dwellings.

Along the valley you will see signs pointing to *Habitations troglodytes* wherever there is a chalk cliff. Most are used for storage but some, as at Troo, are inhabited. Up the hill is the Ancienne Collégiale St Martin, originally eleventh-century and added to in later centuries. North of Troo is the Grand Puits, a deep and echoing roofed-over well, while in Rue Basse is the Grotte Pétrifiante whose stalactites and petrified objects can be visited. On the other side of the river is the little Church of St Jacques-de-Guérets whose fine twelfth-century murals of the Life of Christ have a Byzantine aspect. The most impressive of these is the large *Descent into Hell.*

Both Troo and Montoire, 7km (5 miles) away, were stations on the pilgrimage routes to St James of Compostela in Spain and to the tomb of St Martin in Tours which is why both had lazar-houses. Other than the views, the ruined keep at **Montoire** holds little interest. The most pleasant sight is from the bridge over the Loir. This provides a view of placid water, weeping willows, old house-fronts, boats and fishermen. Chapelle St Gilles, once part of a Benedictine priory of which Ronsard had been the titular head, also has twelfth- and thirteenth-century frescoes. Again, a Byzantine influence appears in the postures, shape of the eyes and rays of light streaming from Christ's hands on to the heads of the Apostles.

Across the river is the romantic ruin of the eleventh-century castle of **Lavardin**, seated on a chalk promontory. Three concentric rings of defensive walls enclosed some 12 acres. The square keep still stands, as do remains of towers and defence works round the drawbridge,

Boating on the River Sarthe at Malicorne

and some vaults of later buildings. Henry II of England and his son Richard Coeur-de-Lion laid unsuccessful siege to Lavardin in 1188. In 1448 the Treaty of Lavardin was signed here between Charles VII and the English.

Yet more wall-paintings (some frescoes, others distemper) are in the Church of St Genest in Lavardin's Grande Rue. In this very early archaic Romanesque building are particularly well-preserved twelfth- to sixteenth-century works which were brought to light in 1914. In Rue de la Barrière some fifteenth-century half-timbered houses have survived. Most publicised of all troglodyte houses are those at **Les Roches-l'Evêque** on the road to Vendôme. Doors and windows decorated with flowers front the houses which are built entirely in the warm chalk cliff. Chapelle St Nicolas (twelfth-century), on the Vendôme road, was once a lazar-house. **Lunay**, 4km (3 miles) beyond Les Roches-l'Evêque on the D53, has a large church with frescoes dating from the fourteenth and fifteenth centuries.

A little detour after Lunay takes in the attractive village of **Mazangé.** It then passes the Manoir de Bonaventure (this is associated with the family of the poet Alfred de Musset), before heading to **Le Gué-du-Loir**, a pretty spot where the Boulon Stream flows into the Loire.

From here, go past Villiers church (this has sixteenth-century wall paintings), and you will come to **Vendôme** by pleasant minor roads. Vendôme is a town of over 18,000 inhabitants. It began life as a Gaulish village, then became *Vindocinum* — the latter's Gallo-Roman remains were excavated 2km (1 mile) upstream. It was pillaged by the English in 1361 and inherited by the Bourbons.

Once the outlying sprawl has been penetrated, the Old Town has a number of buildings which are worthy of a visit. In Place St Martin stands the fifteenth-century Cloche St Martin, the only remnant of a church destroyed in 1856. Situated in a row of old mansions, Hôtel du Saillant (fifteenth-century) was owned by the du Bellay family. It was later to become the infirmary of the school whose rigid discipline Balzac hated so much. La Montagne is the rather elevated name given to the high ground on which the château stands. From it, you can return to the heart of Vendôme by Faubourg St Lubin which crosses the river under the handsome Renaissance Porte St Georges.

The chief attraction is the one-time Abbaye de la Trinité and its free-standing twelfth-century belfry. This is square at the base and ends in an octagon supporting a spire and a cross; it is 80m (250ft) high. Stained glass, statuary and carved misericord choir-stalls are in the church. Attached to the conventual buildings is a museum which concentrates on religious and artisanal work of the region as well as on its local archaeology.

From Vendôme, both Blois and Tours can be easily reached, whilst the river begins to swing northwards. Just on the opposite bank to Vendôme is **Areines**, whose twelfth-century church's interior is covered with some fine frescoes. Stay on this side of the river for the quiet lanes through Fréteval and Cloyes to Châteaudun. An alternative, quicker route is to take the N10, which runs directly to Châteaudun.

Châteaudun originally belonged to the Counts of Blois, and so is historically part of the Loire Valley. The town was laid out to a regular pattern after a fire in the eighteenth century. Only a small area of old houses remains, between the church and the château. The château towers over the River Loir and has been carefully restored. There is a tall twelfth-century keep, but the majority of the buildings date from the fifteenth and sixteenth centuries. The interior is particularly well-furnished, including some fine tapestries. The Sainte Chapelle, adjoining the keep, has some delightful life-size statues of saints. The large square in the centre of the town (Place du 18 Octobre) is host to a lively market every Thursday.

Châteaudun is not far from Orléans, for those who need to complete a long round trip and head northwards to Paris. Angers can be regained either by taking the A10 motorway to Tours, then main roads, or by going north, taking the A11 motorway to Le Mans, then the N23 to Angers.

Although many guide books to the Loire Valley regard Angers as the westernmost point of the Valley, this argument disregards the fact that for many years Angers was the heart of Anjou. Whilst Anjou warred from time to time with its eastern neighbours, the greatest fear lay to the west, and with the powerful Dukes of Brittany. So a more accurate place to end the Loire Valley is where the old border between Anjou and Brittany lay. Although that border moved occasionally, the 'Key to Brittany' was always Ancenis, about halfway between Angers and Nantes.

The old main road, the N23, has been superseded for many by the new A11 motorway. The much quieter route lies on the south side of the river, often hugging the escarpments, and passing through small villages. However, despite its size, the N23 passes some interesting places. Just before St Georges-sur-Loire, 16km (10 miles) from Angers, turn off the road to visit the **Château de Serrant**. Serrant combines both the dark shale and white tufa, and it is surprising to learn that the château was built over a period of some 300 years. It has a harmonious feel to it; the interior is extremely well-maintained and is very well-furnished with tapestries and a fine library. Serrant is close St Georges-sur-Loire, from where some of Anjou's finest wines originate.

Shortly after St Germain-des-Prés there is a ruined castle, all that remains of one built by Gilles de Rais (or de Retz), a notorious character who, having lost a fortune, turned to black magic to try to regain it. He was the inspiration for the fairytale figure of Bluebeard. **Ingrandes** has some pleasant houses overlooking its former quaysides, and is worth a final pause before continuing to Ancenis.

As the main two cities of Angers and Nantes both lay on the north bank of the Loire, the main traffic used (and still uses) that side as the major communications axis. As a result, the meandering roads on the south bank make a very pleasant tail end to the Loire Valley. Leave Angers on Pont de Cé's old road and bridge, rather than the modern one, and turn right at Rabaut on to the D751, which runs all the way to Ancenis. The views across the Loire, with its many sandbanks and islands, show how close the river is getting to the sea.

After Rochefort-sur-Loire, the road is called the Corniche Angevine. It is cut into the cliffs overlooking the flood plain, and commands some surprisingly striking views. The road becomes less dramatic after Chalonnes, although there is still pleasant countryside around. There is a particularly good view of Ingrandes, on the opposite bank. The town itself is easily reached across the bridge.

St Florent-le-Vieil has some pretty views from the shady square in which the church stands. The road swings inland for a short time to avoid previously marshy land, and then joins with the D763 to cross the Loire and enter Ancenis. The strategic importance of Ancenis as a border town is clearly visible in its château, despite the later additions (only open in summer). There is a very pleasant old quarter to stroll around; and there is no better way to end the day in Ancenis than sitting in a café, with a glass of local Muscadet, contemplating the Loire sweeping down its valley to the sea.

Tips for Travellers

Planning Your Visit

Climate

Generally speaking, the Loire has a moderate climate, as the Atlantic Ocean's influence reaches up the Loire, although the summer months can be extremely warm. Spring is temperate with occasional showers and the odd storm or two. In summer the countryside relaxes into a languid stupor, with long, fine days. Summer merges gently into autumn, making this an ideal touring time. Winter tends, on the whole, to be moderate, although the river itself swells and darkens as the rains and snows of the highlands empty themselves upstream.

Weather Information: Loire Valley

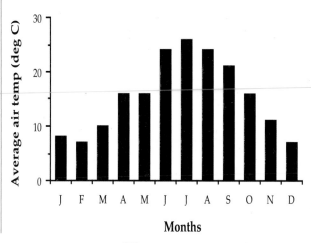

Currency and Credit Cards

Visitors may have as much ready cash as they like when they arrive in France but bank notes and coins should be declared on entry if 50,000 francs or more of notes are likely to be taken out upon departure. It is also worth remembering that banks give a better rate of exchange.

All major credit cards (Mastercard, Visa, American Express etc) are taken at most large restaurants, hotels, shops and garages. Eurocheques and traveller's cheques are also widely accepted.

Visa and to a slightly lesser extent Mastercard (Access), can now be used to pay motorway tolls. Usually, no signature is required.

Customs Regulations

Normal EEC customs regulations apply for those travelling from Britain. Normal European regulations apply for those travelling from North America.

Disabled Visitors

More and more places in France are providing facilities for disabled visitors. Several of the larger towns set aside special parking bays for motorists displaying disabled discs on their vehicles.
Useful addresses to contact are:

Comité National Français de Liaison pour la Réadaption des Handicapés (CNFLRH)
38 Boulevard Raspail
75007 Paris ☎ 45 48 90 13

The Royal Association for Disability and Rehabilitation
25 Mortimer Street
London
W1N 8AB ☎ 071 637 5400

The French Government Tourist Office will supply special information lists on request, including details of hotels which are suitable for guests who are confined to wheelchairs. A stamped, addressed envelope must be enclosed.

Health Care

British travellers have a right to claim health services in France by virtue of EEC regulations. Form E111 — available from the Department of Health and Social Security — should be obtained to avoid complications.

American and Canadian visitors will need to check the validity of their personal health insurance policies to guarantee they are adequately covered. For emergency assistance, dial 17 in all towns. In country areas it may be necessary to phone the local *gendarmerie* (police). Pharmacies, clearly marked with a green cross, can usually deal with minor ailments or advise people where to go if any additional help is needed.

Regardless of the cover, visitors have to pay for treatment at the time and then claim it back. In the event of a serious emergency, contact your insurers who will arrange matters; treatment should not be delayed. For minor ailments involving medical attention you pay the doctor (who will issue a claim form) and the pharmacy (stick the price labels from any medicines to the claim form). You then reclaim the amount following the instructions on the form. Note that a claim takes some time to process, and any refund will usually be forwarded to you.

Motor Insurance

The Green Card is no longer obligatory but full comprehensive cover is advisable. It is as well to check with the motoring organisations or your broker.

Passports

British nationals only need an ordinary valid passport or a British Visitors Passport which is valid for one year. With a few minor exceptions in Europe, the nationals of every country other than those in the EEC need a visa as well.

Travel

As the River Loire runs horizontally across a substantial part of Northern France, and is within easy striking distance of Paris, it is very easily reached, no matter which method of transport is used. In order to get about easily, some form of independent transport is needed, although it is possible to visit the main sights on set tours.

Air

There are few international flights into the region, and no intercontinental flights. The best way is to fly into Paris and transfer to one of the domestic airlines for the internal flights (this may entail a change of airport at Paris). The main Paris airport, the Charles de Gaulle, has excellent international and intercontinental links. It is also alongside the A1 *autoroute* and has good rail and coach links into the centre of Paris.

There are flights twice a week during the season from London Gatwick to Tours. Tours is the main regional airport in the area. Details of flights are available from travel agents or from the French Government Tourist Office.

Bus and Coach

France has few long-distance coaches, but local bus services operate in most large towns and between villages. Local tourist offices can supply timetables and information.

Special tours and excursions within the Loire Valley are widely available from all the major towns throughout the holiday season. Several tours also operate from Paris itself. A number of British tour operators also offer complete coach package tours of the valley and its principal sights. Regional and local tourist offices can supply details of tours, which are generally run by local coach companies. Most will be accompanied but check whether English translation is available if this is required. It is also worth checking whether entry fees and/or meals are included in the price. It is advisable to book in advance.

Railways
It is possible to buy a ticket covering both a flight to Paris and onward travel by rail. As the major sights of the Loire are relatively close to Paris, onward rail travel from the capital is worth considering. The Gare d'Austerlitz is the main terminus for the Valley, although trains for Angers depart from Montparnasse and for Gien from the Gare de Lyon. There is also a regular service from Caen to Tours.

French Railways operate a range of services, and full details can be obtained from their office at 179 Piccadilly, London W1V 0BA (☎ 071 409 3518), or from any travel agent. There is a new high-speed train (TGV) service from Paris to Tours, taking less than 1 hour. TGV trains are all first-class and carry a supplementary charge. Other express services run regularly to Orléans and Tours (around twenty a day in each direction), with slower trains stopping at other towns en route.

It is important to remember that any rail ticket must be stamped (*composter*) in the orange-coloured machines at the entrance to the platform. This validates the ticket and without it a surcharge will be levied by the guard.

Road
Driving is by far the best way to explore the Valley. Driving in France presents few problems as long as the driver remembers the basic rules and regulations — most importantly, to drive on the right. This will need conscious effort to begin with, but soon becomes easier.

Travelling from the North-East and Paris there is the A10 toll motorway for fast access to the Valley. This begins on the Paris ring-road (the Boulevard Périphérique) thus linking it to the main motorways from the Channel Ports, and Paris Charles-de-Gaulle airport. There is also an excellent network of trunk roads all over France, and access to the Loire Valley is straightforward from all of the Channel Ports. The standard of road surface is fairly good on main roads; it is quite easy to average 80kph (50mph).

Remember that French motorways are toll roads — keep a supply of small change or a credit card handy. Fuel is available almost everywhere, although it is advisable to have enough in the tank before heading into the more sparsely populated areas, especially if you are hoping to pay with a credit card.

Always use 'Super' grade petrol. Unleaded fuel (*sans plomb*) is becoming more widely available, especially in towns and on main routes. Cars can be hired in the larger cities and the CSNCRA, 6 Rue Leonardo-de-Vinci, Paris, publishes a list of members who can supply most, if not all, the popular makes. Taxis can only be picked up from a rank or ordered by telephone. They all have meters but the price for an out-of-town trip should be agreed with the driver at the start of the journey to avoid any unnecessary arguments later. You must expect to tip the driver about 15 per cent of the fare.

Motoring
The speed limits currently applied to French roads are:

	In dry conditions	In the wet
Motorways	130kph (81mph)	110kph (68mph)
National (N) roads	110kph (68mph)	90kph (56mph)
Other roads	90kph (56mph)	80kph (50mph)
In towns	60kph (37mph)	60kph (37mph)

Although all the rules of the road must be observed, there are a few which are particularly important. The 60kph (37mph) speed limit for built-up areas comes into force as soon as you enter a town or village (that is, on passing the town or village sign). Motorists can be stopped for a breath test anywhere, at any time. Heavy fines are imposed for being over the limit and they have to be paid in cash on the spot; do not forget to obtain a receipt for these. There are also on-the-spot fines for speeding.

Drivers must be over 18 and hold a valid licence, not a provisional one; no children under 10 years old are allowed on the front seat and safety belts are compulsory. A sign that has a yellow diamond with a white border means that particular road has priority. A black diagonal line through the diamond means that vehicles coming from the right now have right of way (*priorite à droite*).

Every car must have spare bulbs, especially for head-lights. Although red triangles are not obligatory for vehicles equipped with hazard warning lights, it is as well to have them in case of an electrical failure or to give plenty of warning to oncoming traffic if their vision is obscured. Dipped headlights must be used in all built-up areas between dusk and daybreak and sounding the horn is forbidden except in an emergency. Stop signs mean exactly what they say and it is an offence to edge slowly up to the line and then move off, even if there is nothing coming in either direction.

Special Routes
The historical links of the Valley mean that the regional and local tourist offices have developed special tours or routes with different themes. Generally speaking, these are not signposted, but are detailed in leaflets from the tourist offices. This gives visitors as much flexibility as they want. Most feature the châteaux, or well-known historical figures connected with the region, ranging from the great châteaux builders to the Plantagenets. There are a number of nature trails in the Sologne, and local tourist offices have details of these.

Other Means of Travel
There are several other ways of exploring the countryside. Bicycles can be hired in a dozen or more different centres and there are recommended cycle tracks of varying lengths plus overnight stops where necessary. Many cycle shops hire out bicycles for fixed periods. Some of them arrange itineraries for one or two weeks with fixed departure dates in July, August and September. Some

involve visits to châteaux and vineyards. French Railways operate an excellent system of trains which will carry bicycles (usually free of charge) and they can supply full details of these services.

Riding stables provide horses and ponies for short outings or longer expeditions, using bridle paths which also call in at convenient *logis* and *auberges*. Riding holidays include visits to châteaux. Departmental Loisirs-Accueil offices will supply details and make bookings.

Horse-drawn caravans are available for anyone with a taste for the gipsy life. They vary in size and hold from four to ten people. Little rustic carriages can be hired for the day and there are even some places where walkers may find a donkey to carry some of their luggage. Kayaks and canoes are available on all the main rivers, either for an hour or two or for longer trips, in which case there are waterside hamlets and campsites offering food and accommodation.

The long-distance (Grandes Randonnées) and the shorter, blazed footpaths cater for long distance hikers and enthusiastic ramblers as well as people who only want to do a small part of the journey on foot. Local tourist offices often have details of local walks and rambles for the less energetic.

Maps
Both Michelin and IGN produce good maps of the region. Michelin's yellow maps (1cm = 2km) are widely available, accurate and up-to-date: map numbers 63, 64, 65, 67 and 68 cover the area of this book. The IGN Serie Rouge (red) maps (1cm = 2.5km) are also accurate, but with more emphasis on tourist attractions. Those exploring an area in more detail may prefer the IGN blue maps (4cm = 1km). These are large scale, detailed maps. Walkers will want to obtain the appropriate Topo-guide if they want to follow one of the Grandes Randonnées.

When You Are There

Electricity

220 volt electricity is available almost everywhere and plugs are two-pin or very occasionally three-pin, both types are round. Some small areas are still at 110 volt electricity. Adaptors will be needed by those people who do not use continental two-pin plugs at home.

Markets

Open-air markets are held in towns and villages throughout the region, usually once, or sometimes twice a week. They are busy, colourful and interesting, quite apart from the fact that nearly everything one needs is instantly available. The farm produce is seasonal and beautifully fresh. Everything is on sale from clothes and shoes to flowers and kitchenware, at very competitive prices.

Metrication

1 kilo (1,000 grams) — 2.2lb
1 litre — $1\frac{3}{4}$ pints
4.54 litres — 1 gallon
8km — 5 miles

Opening Hours

Banks are open on weekdays from 9am-12noon and again from 2-4pm but they are closed for the day on either Saturdays or Mondays. They also close early on the day before a bank holiday.

Generally speaking, post offices open at 8am-7pm from Monday to Friday but have half a day off from

12noon on Saturdays. However, it is possible that a small country post office may also close for lunch. It is useful to know that stamps (timbres) are on sale in most newsagents and some of the hotels.

Shopping hours also tend to vary somewhat but the usual practice is to open at 9am, close for lunch at 12noon, reopen at 2pm and remain open until 6.30pm or even up to an hour later. Large shops in the cities may stay open throughout the lunch hours and supermarkets seldom close before 9pm or 10pm at night. However, a great many shops of all descriptions are closed on Mondays, either in the morning or for the whole of the day. Some food shops, especially bakers, open on Sunday mornings for a few hours and there is an occasional Sunday market but they are quite few and far between.

Public Holidays

There are eleven public holidays in France when all the banks, administrative offices and most museums are closed although an occasional shop and several restaurants may be open. They are:
New Year's Day
Easter Monday
Labour Day (1 May)
Ascension Day (6 weeks after Easter)
V.E. Day (8 May)
Whit Monday (10 days after Ascension Day)
Bastille Day (14 July)
Assumption Day (15 August)
All Saints' Day (1 November)
Armistice Day (11 November)
Christmas Day

Souvenirs

Wines make for a very pleasant souvenir. However, be prepared for them to be less evocative when drunk at home. Tapestry copies of those in the châteaux are a different souvenir, but can be expensive.

Away from the main towns, there are many rural craftsmen and artisans, often offering traditional wares that make pleasant souvenirs or gifts. Basketware, jewellery, pottery and similar items are all available. The region also has a wide range of artists, and a painting or a print is an ideal memory.

Telephones

Telephones in France take coins rather than tokens. The dial codes from France are:

Great Britain	19 44
Canada	19 1
USA	19 1

Remember to leave out the first zero of your home country number, eg to dial the French Government Tourist Office in London (071 491 7622) from France, dial 19 44 71491 7622. Many telephone booths now take phonecards; buy the *télécarte* from post offices and where advertised on telephone booths. Calls can be received at phone boxes with a blue bell marked on them. Cheaper rates apply from 10.30pm to 8am every evening and at weekends after 2pm on Saturdays.

Most post offices in towns have a number of telephone booths from which you can phone uninterrupted, and then pay at the end of your call. Ask for a booth number at the counter.

In an Emergency
For emergency assistance, dial 17. This will connect you to the emergency services. In very rural areas, it may be necessary to phone the local *gendarmerie* (police).
In the event of a theft, this should be reported to the local police station. They will complete a form detailing any losses — you will need this if you want to claim on insurance — but be prepared to wait.
If you are arrested then contact the nearest appropriate consul or embassy.

Tipping

Tips (*pourboires*) or service charges are included in the
bill but no-one will object if you leave a little extra to
show appreciation for good service or for any other
reason. This applies to hotels, restaurants, cafés, bars etc.
However, guides, cinema attendants, church caretakers
and other people doing similar jobs do expect to be given
a tip.

Water

French tap water is quite safe to drink but a huge range
of bottled mineral water is also available. Never drink
from a tap marked *Eau non potable*.

FURTHER INFORMATION FOR VISITORS

Information and Booking Centres

National Tourist Offices

The French government supports a network of national tourist offices outside France. These provide general information about the country, travel, transport, and accommodation, usually on a regional basis. They also give details of tour operators providing accommodation, holidays or tours to France. Inevitably, these offices are always very busy, and are rarely able to assist with telephone enquiries, so it is best to call personally, or to write. Remember to enclose a stamped, addressed envelope.

The main French tourist offices are:-

Great Britain
178 Piccadilly
London W1V 0AL
☎ 071 491 7622

USA
610 Fifth Avenue
Suite 222
New York NY 10020 - 2452
☎ 212 757 1683

Canada
1981 Avenue McGill College
Tour Esso Suite 490
Montreal
Quebec H3 A2W9
☎ 514 288 4264

Regional Tourist Boards
Comité Régional du Tourisme du Val de Loire
9 rue St Pierre Lentin
45041 ORLEANS Cedex 1
☎ 38 54 95 42
Telex: 783455

Comité Régional du Tourisme des Pays de la Loire
Maison du Tourisme
Place du Commerce
44000 NANTES
☎ 40 48 24 20

Tourist Boards of *Départements*
These are in order, moving downstream.

Comité Départemental du Tourisme de Cher
10 rue de la Chappe
18014 BOURGES Cedex
☎ 48 65 31 01, Telex: 783368

Comité Départemental du Tourisme de Loiret
2 rue de la Bretonnerie
45000 ORLEANS
☎ 38 54 83 83, Telex: 780 523

Comité Départemental du
Tourisme de Loir-et-Cher
11 place du Château
41000 BLOIS
☎ 54 78 55 50
Telex: 751375

Comité Départemental du
Tourisme d'Indre-et-Loire
16 rue de Buffon
37032 TOURS Cedex
☎ 47 61 61 23
Telex: 751459 (attn: CDT)

Comité Départemental du
Tourisme de Maine-et-Loire
Maison du Tourisme
Place Kennedy
BP 214849021 ANGERS Cedex
☎ 41 88 23 85

Comité Départemental du
Tourisme de Loire-Atlantique
Maison du Tourisme
Place du Commerce
44000 NANTES
☎ 40 89 50 77

Tour Operators

As France is such a popular
destination, many tour operators
offer all sorts of holidays to the
Loire Valley. These range from
straightforward châteaux tours, to
longer stays in hotels or self-
catering accommodation, to a
variety of activity holidays. It is
impossible to list them all here.
Any reputable travel agent will be
able to suggest a selection of
companies, otherwise contact the
French Government Tourist Offices
shown above.

Regional Booking Offices

A number of *départements* have set
up officially backed booking

offices. These all operate under the
common name of Loisirs Accueil.
They are able to make advance
reservations for hotels and self-
catering accommodation, as well as
camping and caravan sites. In
addition, they offer a range of
activity holidays, and can often
help with general enquiries ahead
of arrival. Please note that each
département only makes bookings
for its own area. However, the
service is usually free and almost
every office has at least one
member of staff that speaks
English. Most of the offices are
open Monday to Friday, 9am-
12noon and 2-6pm.

Maine-et-Loire
Maison du Tourisme
Place Kennedy
BP 852
49008 - Angers
☎ 41 88 23 85

Indre-et-Loire
Loisirs Accueil
38 rue Augustin-Fresnel
BP 139
37171 - Chambray Lès Tours
☎ 47 48 37 27
Telex: 750 116

Loir-et-Cher
Loisirs Accueil
11 place du Château
41000 - Blois
☎ 54 78 55 50
Telex: 751 375

Loiret
Loisirs Accueil
3 rue de la Bretonnerie
45000 - Orléans
☎ 38 62 04 88
Telex: 780 523

Cher
Loisirs Accueil
10 rue de la Chappe
18014 - Bourges
☎ 48 70 74 75
Telex: 783 368

Tourist Information Centres
All major tourist towns, as well as numerous smaller places, have a tourist information centre called *Office de Tourisme* or *Syndicat d'Initiative*. At the smaller resorts, these offices are only likely to be open during the summer season. They provide free information about hotels, campsites, local amenities, excursions, special events, museums, châteaux and *son-et-lumière* events, as well as wine-tasting addresses. Local guide books may also be on sale (or ask at the nearest bookshop).

Most of the major tourist offices are open from 9am to 12noon and from 2 to 6pm, Monday to Friday. In the main holiday period these hours are extended, usually to 9am-8pm, and include Saturday. Offices in the major cities like Tours also open on Sunday in the summer months.

Associated with the *Office de Tourisme* in larger towns is *Accueil de France* which makes same-day (and not more than five days in advance) hotel bookings. These facilities are available at:

Angers
Place Kennedy
☎ 41 88 69 93

Blois
Pavillon Anne de Bretagne
3 Avenue Jean Laigret
☎ 54 74 06 49, Telex: 750 135

Orléans
Place Albert I
☎ 38 53 05 95
Telex: 781 188

Tours
Place Maréchal Leclerc
☎ 47 05 58 08
Telex: 750 008

Tourist information offices at other important but smaller tourist centres in the Loire Valley are at:

Amboise
Office de Tourisme
Quai Général de Gaulle
☎ 47 57 09 98

Ancenis
Office de Tourisme
Place du Pont
☎ 40 83 07 44

Aubigny-sur-Nère
Syndicat d'Initiative
Mairie
☎ 48 58 00 09

Azay-le-Rideau
Rue Nationale
☎ 47 45 44 40

Baugé
Hôtel de Ville
☎ 41 89 12 12

Beaugency
Office de Tourisme
28 Place Martroi
☎ 38 44 54 42

Bourges
Office de Tourisme
14 Place E. Dolet
☎ 48 24 75 33
(Although it lies on the Loire Valley's periphery, Bourges is placed in this list because it is a major centre).

Château-du-Loir
Syndicat d'Initiative, Mairie
☎ 43 44 00 38

Châteaudun
1 rue de Luynes
☎ 37 45 22 46

Château-Gontier
Syndicat d'Initiative
Mairie
☎ 43 07 07 10

Châteauneuf-sur-Sarthe
Quai de la Sarthe
☎ 41 69 82 89

Chinon (Indre-et-Loire)
Office de Tourisme
12 rue Voltaire
☎ 47 93 17 85

Doué-la-Fontaine
Syndicat d'Initiative
Place Hôtel-de-Ville
☎ 41 59 20 49

La Flèche
Place du Marché-au-Blé
☎ 43 94 02 53

Fontevraud
Hôtel de Ville
☎ 41 51 71 41

Gien
Office de Tourisme
rue Anne-de-Beaujeu
☎ 38 67 25 28

Langeais
Syndicat d'Initiative
Mairie
☎ 47 96 58 22

Loches
Office de Tourisme
Place Marne
☎ 47 59 07 98

Loudun
Hôtel de Ville
☎ 49 98 15 96

Le Lude
Place F. de-Nicolay
(Easter - September only)
☎ 43 94 62 20

Montreuil-Bellay
Mairie
☎ 41 52 33 86

Montrichard
Office de Tourisme
Mairie
☎ 54 32 00 46

Richelieu
Syndicat d'Initiative
Grande Rue
☎ 47 58 13 62

Romorantin-Lanthenay
Syndicate d'Initiative
Place de la Paix
☎ 54 76 43 89

Sablé-sur-Sarthe
Place Elize
☎ 43 95 00 60

St Aignan
Office de Tourisme
(1 July-31 August)
☎ 54 75 22 85

Saumur
Office de Tourisme
Place de la Bilange
☎ 41 51 03 06

Sully-sur-Loire
Office de Tourisme
Place de Général de Gaulle
☎ 38 35 32 21

Vendôme
Office de Tourisme
Rue Poterie
☎ 54 77 05 07

Son-et-lumière

Son-et-lumière was born in the Loire Valley. The first performances were given at the Château of Chambord in 1952. *Son-et-lumière* has now spread world-wide. Each château presents the theme of its main historical events. Its past life is re-enacted by actors in period costume.

Scenarios, titles and times of performances may alter. Check times of the next performance locally (particularly as the times given in the list which follows are only a very general indication). Up-to-date information is available at the château itself, at the local tourist office, at your hotel, and on street advertisements.

This is not a cheap form of entertainment. Entrance fees are lower for parties than for individuals. Special rates apply for children.

Local coach operators run evening package tours. Again, the local tourist office will have details.

Amboise

A la Cour du Roy François.
A Renaissance party at the royal castle. 420 actors in period costume. On certain dates between end of June and end of August, starting around 10pm (90 mins).
☎ 47 57 14 47

Azay-le-Rideau

Puisque de vous n'avons autre visage.
From last weekend in May to last weekend in September, starting around 10pm (60 mins).
☎ 47 45 44 40

Blois

Les Esprits aiment la nuit.
In French and English. On certain days between end of April to end of September; daily at other times in summer (closed Thursdays except in July and August). English version at 10pm or later (30 mins).
☎ 54 74 06 49

Il etait une fois Louis XII.
An historical pageant of famous people involved with the Château de Blois; certain dates in June, July and August. French language only. 10.30pm (90 mins).
☎ 54 78 55 50

Chambord

Le Combat du jour et de la nuit.
Between late April and end September, starting at 9.30pm or later (35 mins).
☎ 54 20 31 32

Chenonceaux

Aux Temps des Dames de Chenonceau.
(Note: it is correct to spell the village with an 'x' and the château without.) Between mid-June and mid-September, starting at 10pm or later (45 mins).
Information: Château de Chenonceau, Chenonceaux, 37150 Bléré.
☎ 47 23 90 07 or 47 23 93 52

Cheverny (Loir-et-Cher)

Cheverny à la lueur des flambeaux.
On a theme of a Renaissance hunting party. Late July to mid-August (60 mins).
Information: Château de Cheverny, Cheverny, 41700 Contres.
☎ 54 79 96 29

Loches

Charles par la Grace des Femmes.
The evolution of France from Middle Ages to Renaissance in the reign of Charles VII. Certain dates in July and August. Starts 10pm (90 mins).
☎ 47 59 07 98

Le Lude

Les Glorieuses et fastueuses soirées au bord du Loir.
Five centuries of history with 350 actors in period costume, 300 fountains, and fireworks too. Between second weekend in June to first weekend in September, starting around 10pm (105 mins). On Friday and Saturday evenings, fireworks display.
☎ 43 94 62 20

Saché

Balzac et la Vallée du Lys.
A series of tableaux evoking the life and times of Balzac. Certain dates in June and July. 10.30pm (85 mins).
☎ 47 26 86 65

Valençay

La Belle Captive.
Actors, musicians and horsemen in Renaissance costume. Weekends between early July to early September (110 mins).
Information during *son-et-lumière* season:
Syndicat d'Initiative
36600 Valençay
☎ 54 00 04 42
At other times: Château de Valençay
BP 23, 36600 Valençay
☎ 54 00 14 33

Châteaux Open to the Public

The châteaux listed here are mostly those which charge an entrance fee to view them and, in some cases, their gardens as well. A few which can only be viewed from outside the building make no charge. Many more than can be included here are not open to the public but can be glimpsed from the roadside in passing.

The words 'open daily' are to be understood as meaning open both morning and afternoon with about a 2 hour lunch break. In July and August some places remain open continuously throughout the day. Afternoon closing times vary according to the season. Some châteaux are open on French public holidays; most are closed on at least some of them.

In addition, many châteaux close on one weekday (usually Tuesday). All details of opening days and times should be checked locally, as there can be changes at short notice.

Day and evening (the latter for *son-et-lumière*) coach trips to local châteaux during the season are available at many tourist resorts. Some are accompanied by English-speaking guides. Enquire at local tourist offices.

Châteaux, followed by their nearest towns, are listed by *départements*.

CHER

Béthune
La Chapelle d'Angillon
Open: daily except Sunday

morning from Palm Sunday to October.

Guided visits include audio-visual show (10 mins) about Alain-Fournier, author of *Le Grand Meaulnes*, born in La Chapelle d'Angillon. The château inspired his celebrated novel.

☎ 48 73 41 10

Blancafort

Open: daily except Tuesday, mid March to November; and Sunday afternoon, November to December. Guided visits (40 mins). Pamphlets in English.

☎ 48 58 60 56

Boucard

Jars-le-Noyer. 5km (3 miles) south of Jars on D74
Open: daily all year. Pamphlets in English.

☎ 48 58 72 81

Palais Jacques Coeur

Bourges, Rue Jacques Coeur.
Open: daily all year.
☎ 48 24 06 87

Maupas

Morogues, 1km ($^1/_2$ mile) west on D59
Open: daily July to early September; mornings only mid-April to June and early September to mid-October. Guided visit (40 mins).
☎ 48 64 41 71

Menetou-Salon

Open: daily last week in April to November. Pamphlets in English.
☎ 48 64 80 54 or 54 64 80 16

La Verrerie

Oizon. D39 south of Oizon for 6km

(4 miles), left after Les Naudins for 1km ($^1/_2$ mile) on D89
Open: daily mid-February to mid-November. Pamphlets in English.
☎ 48 58 06 91

EURE-ET-LOIRE

Châteaudun

Open: daily, all year. Guided tours (45 mins). Leaflets in English.
☎ 37 45 22 70

INDRE

Valençay

Guided visits (60 mins) daily mid-March to mid-November. Pamphlets in English. Entrance charge includes gardens, zoo and Musée de l'Automobile du Centre (60 vintage cars dating from 1898).
☎ 54 00 14 33

INDRE-ET-LOIRE

Amboise

Guided visits (45 mins) daily all year.
☎ 47 57 00 98

Azay-le-Rideau

Open: daily all year. Pamphlets in English.

Chatigny

Fondettes. On D76, right at Mareuil on D276, and first right.
Open: daily all year to see exterior only.
☎ 47 42 20 05

Chenonceau

Open: daily all year. Snack bar, tea rooms. Children's nursery July to August. Electric train in July and August. Pamphlets in English.

Musée de Cire (Waxwork Museum) in grounds of château, with wax models to illustrate history and personalities connected with château.
☎ 47 23 90 07

Chinon

Open: daily February to November; closed Wednesday. Pamphlets in English. Ticket gives access to Fort St Georges, Château du Milieu, Fort du Coudray.
☎ 47 93 13 45

Cinq Mars-la-Pile

Open: daily all year. Pamphlets in English. Guided visits (30 mins) including park.
☎ 47 96 40 49

Langeais

Open: daily all year except Monday out of season. Guided tours (60 mins). Pamphlets in English.
☎ 47 96 72 60

Leugny

Azay-sur-Cher. 2km (1 mile) east of Azay on N76, and left along drive Guided tours in afternoons from last week in July and August. At other times, groups by previous arrangement.
☎ 47 50 41 10

Loches

Logis Royal.
Open: daily February to November; closed Wednesday out of season. Includes Tour Agnès Sorel, Logis Royaux tomb of Agnès Sorel, triptych of School of Jean Fouquet (fifteenth-century). Pamphlets in English.
☎ 47 90 01 32

Loches

Donjon (keep)
Open: daily February to November; closed Wednesday out of season. Guided visit includes Tour Ronde and Martelet. Pamphlets in English.
☎ 47 59 07 86

Montpoupon

Montrichard. 12km (8 miles) southwest from Montrichard on D764
Open: daily mid-June to September.
☎ 47 94 23 62

Montrésor

Guided visits (30 mins) daily April to October. Pamphlets in English.
☎ 47 92 60 04

Plessis-lès-Tours

Guided visits (60 mins) daily except Tuesday and public holidays, February to December. Pamphlets in English.
☎ 47 37 22 80

Réaux

Bourgueil. South on D749 for 4km (3 miles) to Les Réaux, right to far end of village.
Group visits by previous arrangement.
☎ 47 95 14 40

Rivau

Champigny-sur-Veude. 4km (3 miles) north on D749 to Le Coudray, first left off D114
Guided visits (60 mins) daily mid-March to October.
☎ 142 00 20 99

Saché

Open: daily February to Novem-

ber; closed Wednesday February to mid-March, and October to November. Pamphlets in English.
☎ 47 26 86 50

Ste Maure-de-Touraine
Open: daily except Sunday mid-June to mid-September. At other times groups by previous arrangement. Commentaries in English.
☎ 47 65 66 35

Ussé
Rigny-Ussé
Guided visits (45 mins) daily mid-March to November. Pamphlets in English.
☎ 47 95 54 05

Vaudésir Manoir
St Christophe-sur-le-Nais
Open: daily all year except Monday.
☎ 47 29 24 53

Villandry
Guided visits (40 mins) daily of château interior, mid-March to mid-November. Commentaries in English. (For garden, see Wildlife, Zoos and Gardens section.)

LOIR-ET-CHER

Beauregard
Cellettes. Just north of village
Open: daily all year, but closed Wednesdays early February to March and October to December. Guided visits (30 mins). Pamphlets in English. Includes Galerie des Illustres (historical portraits), Cabinet des Grelots (sixteenth-century room) and sixteenth-century kitchen.
☎ 54 70 40 05

Blois
Open: daily all year. Guided visits (60 mins). Pamphlets in English available. Audio-visual performances in season. Entrance charge includes St Saturnin cemetery, Musée des Beaux Arts, Musée Archéologique.

Chambord
Open: daily January to December. Pamphlets in English.
☎ 54 20 31 32

Chaumont-sur-Loire
Open: daily January to December. Guided visits (30 mins) include stables and park. Only park can be visited.
☎ 54 78 19 47 and 54 46 98 03

Chémery
Furnished apartments.
Open: daily all year. Pamphlets in English.
☎ 54 71 82 77

Cheverny
Cour-Cheverny
Open: daily all year. Guided tours available. Pamphlets in English.
☎ 54 79 96 29

La Ferté-Imbault
Open: afternoons Monday, Saturday, Sunday, July to September. Commentaries (45 mins) in English.
☎ Paris 1 622 47 26

Fougères-sur-Bièvre
Open: daily all year except Tuesday and Wednesday and public holidays. 30 mins.
☎ 54 78 19 47

Gué-Péan
Monthou-sur-Cher
Guided visits (45 mins) of furnished rooms daily all year. Commentaries in English.

Ménars
Temporarily closed for restoration at time of writing.

Montoire-sur-le-Loir
Square eleventh-century keep. Apply to Syndicat d'Initiative, Mairie (☎ 54 85 38 63) which is open daily except Sunday, July to mid-September, for arrangement to view. Model of original château in Mairie.

Montrichard
Keep
Open: daily early June to early September, and Saturday and Sunday only mid-April to early June, mid-September to November. 20 mins. Pamphlets in English.
☎ 54 32 05 10

Le Moulin
Lassay-sur-Croisne. 1.5km (1 mile) west of Lassay
Guided tours (30 mins) daily March to mid-November.
☎ 54 83 83 51

St Denis-sur-Loire
Open: daily except Sunday January to September to view exterior only.
☎ 54 78 31 02

Selles-sur-Cher
Open: daily July to mid-September, and afternoons of Saturday and Sunday mid-September to June. Closed mid-November to Easter.
☎ 54 97 59 10

Talcy
Guided visits (30 mins) daily except Tuesday, January to December, includes furnished apartments and their tapestries, pigeon-loft, and 400-year-old wine press.
☎ 54 78 19 47

Troussay
Cour-Cheverny. D52 south-west of Cour-Cheverny, right fork after 3km (2 miles).
Guided visits (25 mins) daily last week in March to mid-April, and May to mid-September; Sunday and public holidays only last two weeks in April and mid-September to mid-November. Includes collection of traditional agricultural implements of Sologne.
☎ 54 44 29 07

Vendôme
Open: daily except Tuesday March to November. Separate charges for château and gardens.
☎ 54 77 01 33

Villesavin
Tour-en-Sologne 3km (2 miles) west of Bracieux on D102, right at Ponts-d'Arian, cross River Beuvron, right along drive. Guided visits (40 mins) daily March to September, and afternoons only October to mid-December. Pamphlets in English.
☎ 54 46 42 88

LOIRET

Beaugency
Château Dunois. Guided visits (90 mins) daily all year, but closed Tuesday. Includes Musée Régional

des Arts et Traditions de
l'Orléannais.
☎ 38 44 55 23

Châteauneuf-sur-Loire
Daily visits all year to view exterior
and gardens, arboretum, giant
rhododendrons.
☎ 38 58 41 18

Gien
Guided visits (90 mins) daily all
year, includes Musée International
de la Chasse (Museum of the
History of Hunting).
☎ 38 67 24 11

La Ferté-St Aubin
West on D61 from La Ferté, lane off
right for 1km ($^1/_2$ mile).
Open: daily mid-March to
November, exterior only.
☎ 38 76 52 72

Meung-sur-Loire
Guided visits (60 mins) in English
daily mid-March to mid-November. Entrance charges for both
château and underground
oubliettes.
☎ 38 44 36 47 or 38 44 25 61

Orléans
Hôtel Groslot, Place de l'Etape
Open: daily all year except
Saturday mornings. Pamphlets in
English.
☎ 38 42 22 30

Sully-sur-Loire
Guided visits (60 mins) daily
March to November.
☎ 38 36 25 60

MAINE-ET-LOIRE

Angers
Open: daily all year except public
holidays. Entrance fee includes
access to Musée Lurçat, Musée des
Beaux-Arts, Musée Pincé and
cathedral treasury. Pamphlets in
English.
☎ 41 88 69 93

Baugé
Château du Roi René
Open: daily June to September.
☎ 41 89 12 12

Boumois
St Martin-de-la-Place. 1km ($^1/_2$
mile) south-east of St Martin, off
D952
Open: daily except Tuesday, Easter
to All Saints' Day.
☎ 41 38 43 16

Coudray-Montbault
St Hilaire-du-Bois. 3km (2 miles)
north-west on D254 beyond
crossroads with N160
Open: daily July to September.
☎ 41 75 80 47

Brissac
Guided visits (60 mins) daily
except Tuesday.
☎ 41 91 22 13

Manoir de la Harmonière
Champigné. D768 south for 1.5km
(1 mile), left
Open: daily July to mid-September.
☎ 41 42 01 38

La Lorie
Segré. 2km (1 mile) south of Segré
on D961
Guided visits (30 mins) afternoons

July to mid-September; closed Tuesday. Pamphlets in English.
☎ 41 92 10 04

Montgeoffroy
Mazé. 2km (1 mile) north-west of Mazé on D74
Open: daily Palm Sunday to All Saints' Day.
☎ 41 80 60 02

Montreuil-Bellay
Guided visits (45 mins) daily except Tuesday April to October and daily including Tuesday July to August. Commentaries in English.
Only gardens can be visited.
☎ 41 52 33 06

Montsoreau
Guided visits (60 mins) daily except Tuesday all year.
☎ 41 51 70 25

La Perrière
Avrillé. From Angers on N162, right at Avrillé for 0.5km ($1/_4$ mile)
Open: daily except Wednesday July to mid-September.
☎ 41 69 20 17

Le Plessis-Bourré
Ecuillé. D74 west from Ecuillé, right on D508 for 1.5km (1 mile).
Guided visits (45 mins) daily all year except Wednesday, Thursday and Sunday mornings.
☎ 41 32 06 01

Le Plessis-Macé
Guided visits (60 mins) daily except Tuesday July to September; at other times afternoons only. Closed December to February.

Les Ponts-de-Cé
Open: daily except Monday April to September.

Raguin
Chazé-sur-Argos. Just north of village. Open: daily mid-May to mid-September afternoon only.

Serrant
St Georges-sur-Loire. N23 towards Angers, right in 1km ($1/_2$ mile)
Guided visits (45 mins) daily April to October. Closed Tuesday except July and August; furnished apartments included.

Saumur
Open: daily April to October, and daily except Tuesday, November to March. Guided visits (60 mins) in English. Entrance fee includes Musée des Arts Decoratifs and Musée du Cheval.
☎ 41 51 03 06

SARTHE

Bazouges-sur-le Loir
Open: Saturday afternoon from Easter Saturday to June; Tuesday morning, Thursday and Saturday afternoon, July to mid-September.
☎ 43 94 30 67

Courtanvaux
Bessé-sur-Braye. 1km ($1/_2$ mile) north of Bessé
Open: daily, May to September at 10, 11am and 2, 3, 4, 5, 6pm when there are at least six persons in a group. Closed Tuesday. Rest of year, open Sundays and public holidays at the same times. In summer, art exhibitions, concerts and plays.

Poncé-sur-le-Loir
Open: daily all year except Sunday
morning, for visit of château,
gardens and pigeon-loft.
☎ 43 44 45 31

La Possonière
Couture-sur-Loir. Manor house lies
0.5km ($^1/_4$ mile) south of Couture
Private property, but grounds of
birthplace of poet Ronsard may be
visited during absence of owners,
and by prior arrangement.

Museums and Buildings of Special Interest

For information about opening
times see introduction to Châteaux
Open to the Public section.

CHER

Bourges
Cathedral crypt and tower
Audio-visual 'Trésors d' Art du
Cher', daily except Sunday
morning, last week in April to
October. (35 mins)

Musée du Berry
Hôtel Cujas, 4 Rue des Arènes
Social history, archaeology of
province.
Open: daily except Tuesday and
public holidays.
☎ 48 70 41 92

Hôtel Lallemant
6 Rue Bourbonnoux
Art collection.
Open: daily except Monday and
Sunday mornings, 2 January to 24
December.
☎ 48 57 81 17

Musée d'Histoire Naturelle
Rue Messire Jacques
Natural history collections.
Open: all year, afternoon only.
☎ 48 57 82 44

Guided tours of old quarters,
starting at Office de Tourisme, 14
Place E. Dolet. Pamphlets in
English.
☎ 48 24 75 33

Nançay
Observatoire de Radioastronomie
Radioastronomy centre. Commentaries in English.
Open: daily all year to groups by
previous arrangement.
☎ 48 51 82 41

Grenier de Villâtre
Exhibition of work by group of
artists.
Open: Saturdays and Sundays.

Vierzon
Musée des Amis du Vieux Vierzon
Rue du Château
Porcelain exhibition.
☎ 48 71 47 86

INDRE

Chabris
Mairie
Collections of insects and old coins.
Open: Sunday afternoon, July to
August.
☎ 54 40 03 32

Luçay-le-Mâle
Musée de la Pierre à Fusil
Village de Retraite, Rue du Champ
de Foire
Flintlock collection.
☎ 54 40 43 97

INDRE-ET-LOIRE

Amboise
Musée de l'Hôtel de Ville
Rue François I
Local history and paintings.
Open: all year Monday to Friday.
☎ 47 57 02 21

Musée de la Poste
Hôtel de Joyeuse, 6 Rue de Joyeuse
History of early postal services.
Open: daily except Monday.
Pamphlets in English.
☎ 47 57 02 21

Manoir du Clos-Lucé
Rue du Clos-Lucé
Manor house (Tour: 45 mins),
gardens, Leonardo da Vinci
museum with working models of
his inventions. Pamphlets in
English.
Open: daily February to December.
☎ 47 57 62 88

Pagode de Chanteloup
2.5km (1¹/₂ miles) south of Bléré
road
Folly in Chinese style, grounds,
woods.
Pamphlets in English.
Open: daily except Monday all
year.

Avoine
Centrale Nucléaire de Chinon
Chinon nuclear power station
Commentary in English. Viewing
platform.
Open: daily all year.

Station open all year Monday to
Friday to groups by previous
arrangement (minimum notice, 2
weeks).
☎ 47 98 97 07

Bourgueil
Benedictine Abbey
Guided tours from Easter to
September on Sunday afternoon
and public holidays, as well as
Friday to Monday, July to August
(60 mins).
☎ 47 97 72 04

Champigny-sur-Veude
Chapelle du Château
Commentaries (40 mins) in
English. Groups by previous
arrangement daily for rest of year.
Sixteenth-century stained-glass
windows.
Open: daily April to early November.
☎ 47 95 71 46

Chinon
Musée du Vieux Chinon
Maison des Etats Généraux
44 Rue Haute St Maurice
Museum of local curios.
Open: daily except Tuesday and
January and February.
☎ 47 93 17 85

*Musée des Arts et Traditions
Populaires*
Chapelle Ste Radegonde
Guided visits by previous arrangement daily, June to mid-August.
Commentaries in English.
☎ 47 93 17 85

Tour of Old Town, starting from
Office de Tourisme
12 rue Voltaire
Daily all year (90 mins). Groups by
previous arrangement.
☎ 47 93 17 85

La Devinière
Cross River Vienne by D749, right
on D751, and follow signs

Birthplace of Rabelais and museum.
Pamphlets in English.
Open: daily March to September; daily except Wednesday in February, October, and November

Cormery
Abbey
Only remains of cloisters can be visited.
☎ 47 43 30 84

Cravant-les-Coteaux
Musée du Vieux-Cravant
Mairie
Lapidary museum.
Open: afternoons only (closed Tuesday) all year.
☎ 47 93 12 40

L'Ile-Bouchard
Prieuré St Léonard
Apply to house next door to see carved capitals on four columns in twelfth-century church.

Loches
Nocturnal tour of Old Town, starting from Pavillon du Tourisme, Place Marne.
At 9.30pm daily, July to mid-September (90 mins). Commentaries in English. Groups by previous arrangement daily during rest of year.
☎ 47 59 07 98

Mussée Lansyer et Musée du Terroir
Rue Lansyer
Reconstructed nineteenth-century Touraine house. Local costumes, arms, historical objects.
Open: daily. Guided visits July to mid-September all year (75 mins).
Pamphlets in English.
☎ 47 59 05 45

Abbey church at Beaulieu-lès-Loches, 1km ($^1/_2$ mile) east.
Apply to Mairie for guided tours in summer, or ask for key at 2 Rue Foulques Nerra.

Luzé
Abbaye de Bois Aubry
Twelfth-century Benedictine abbey 3km (2 miles) south-east of Luzé, left off D110
Open: daily all year except during services. Commentaries in English.
☎ 47 58 34 48

Meslay
Parçay-Meslay
Medieval tithe barn
Audio-visual show, *Un pilier de la grange raconte…*
Pamphlets in English. Art exhibitions, auditorium for Touraine Music Festival (last weekend in June, first weekend in July).
Open: afternoon only, Saturday, Sunday and public holidays, late April to October.
☎ 47 29 19 29

Montrésor
Chartreuse du Liget
6km (4 miles) west of Montrésor on D760
Exterior only can be viewed daily. To see over Carthusian buildings (privately owned) enquire at door on left of main courtyard.
☎ 47 94 20 02

Chapelle St Jean du Liget
6.5km (4 miles) west of Montrésor on D760, left along lane and right along rough track.
To obtain key to twelfth-century circular chapel, ask at Chartreuse du Liget (above).

Négron

2km (1 mile) west of Amboise on N152. Twelfth-century barn. Art exhibitions in summer.

Richelieu

Musée de l'Hôtel de Ville
History of town.
Open: daily except Tuesday and weekends, January to June; daily except Tuesday, July to August; daily except Tuesday and week-ends, September to December.
☎ 47 58 10 13

St Etienne-de-Chigny

11km (7 miles) west of Tours on N152, right
Sixteenth-century church with huge, carved grotesque masks on timbers, stained-glass windows. Key obtainable at grocery (closed Mondays) next door.

Savigné-sur-Lathan

Musée du Savignéen
Faubourg de la Rue
Geology museum. Pamphlets in English.
Open: Saturday and Sunday afternoons, mid-March to June and September to mid-November; every afternoon except Thursday, July to August.
☎ 47 24 95 14

Savonnières

Caves Pétrifiantes
Petrified caves. Pamphlets in English.
Guided visits (45 mins) daily except Thursday, February to March and October to mid-December; daily April to mid-September.
☎ 47 50 00 09

Tavant Church

2km (1 mile) outside l'Ile-Bouchard, west on D760, narrow turning on left in village
To view twelfth-century frescoes, see notice-board outside church.

Tours

Daily audio-guided tour round old quarters from Office de Tourisme, Place Maréchal Leclerc (150 mins). Tapes in English.
☎ 47 05 58 08

Visit to old quarters with English-speaking guide available daily all year by previous arrangement.
☎ 47 05 58 08

Musée des Equipages Militaires et du Train
Rue du Plat d'Etain
Museum of the history of military baggage-trains.
Open: all year, afternoons only, Monday to Friday. On Saturday and Sunday open to groups by previous arrangement.
☎ 47 61 44 46, ext 373

Hôtel Mame
19 Rue Emile Zola
Exhibition of silks produced by one-time Tours factories. Pamphlets in English.
Open: afternoons only, April to mid-November.
☎ 47 05 60 87

Musée de Compagnonnage
Cloître St Julien, 8 Rue Nationale
Museum of ancient crafts and tools used by organised *compagnons* (guilds) of craftsmen. Pamphlets in English.
Open: daily all year except Tuesday and public holidays.
☎ 47 61 07 93

Musée Archéologique de Touraine
Hôtel Goüin, 25 Rue du Commerce
Museum of regional archaeology.
Pamphlets in English.
Open: daily except Friday,
February to mid-March, and
October to November; daily mid-
March to September.
☎ 47 66 22 32

Musée du Gemmail
Hôtel Rimbaud, 7 Rue du Mûrier
Museum of pictorial reproductions
by modern techniques.
Open: daily except Monday, March
to mid-October.
☎ 47 61 01 19

Musée des Beaux-Arts
18 Place François-Sicard
Art gallery.
Open: daily except Tuesday.
Closed on public holidays. Guided
tours in English in summer (60
mins).
☎ 47 05 68 73

Historial de la Touraine
Quai d'Orléans
Waxworks museum
Open: daily April to October; open
afternoons only November to
December.
☎ 47 61 02 95

Cloître St Gatien (La Psalette)
Attached to north side of cathedral.
Guided tours daily. Apply to
cathedral caretaker.

St Cosme Priory
Plessis-lès-Tours, 3km (2 miles)
west of centre of Tours on south
side of Loire
Tomb of poet Ronsard. Pamphlets
in English.
Open: daily except Wednesday
February to mid-March and

October to November; daily mid-
March to September.
☎ 47 37 32 70

Turpenay Abbey
In Forêt de Chinon. From Chinon,
D751 towards Azay-le-Rideau; left
after 8km (5 miles), through St
Benoît-la-Forêt and right after 2km
(1 mile)
Open: all day throughout year,
Monday to Friday. Exterior only.
Pamphlets in English.
☎ 47 58 01 47

Villaines-les-Rochers
Société Coopérative Agricole de
Vannerie
Exhibition and sale of long-
established local basket-work
industry.
☎ 47 45 43 03

LOIR-ET-CHER

Blois
Musée Lapidaire
Cloître St Saturnin, Rue Munier
Museum of sculpture
Open: all day Wednesday,
Saturday, Sunday January to mid-
March and November to Decem-
ber; all day Wednesday to Sunday
mid-March to October.
☎ 54 74 06 49

Hôtel d'Alluye
Italian Renaissance courtyard and
galleries can be visited during
office hours.

Chocolaterie Poulain
To arrange visit (75 mins) to factory
☎ 54 78 39 21 ext 339

Blois historique
Visits to old quarters from the
château.

Daily except Wednesday and Sunday, mid-June to mid-September. Groups daily during rest of year by previous arrangement.
☎ 54 74 16 06

La Chaussée-St Victor
Musée Adrien Thiebault
116 Rue Nationale, on eastern outskirts of Blois
Small museum of Naive ceramics, dolls and models reconstructing local scenes.

Gy-en-Sologne
Locature de la Straize
13km (8 miles) west of Romorantin-Lanthenay on D59
Agricultural museum.
Open: daily except Saturday and Sunday, mid-March to mid-November.
☎ 54 83 82 89

Lassay-sur-Croisne
11km (7 miles) west of Romorantin-Lanthenay on D59 and D20
Fifteenth-century church with sixteenth-century frescoes. Enquire at Town Hall.

Lanthenay
Enquire for key at house opposite Calvary on D922, to see sixteenth-century paintings and wooden statues in the church.

Maves
Moulin-à-vent
17km (10 miles) along Blois to Châteaudun road, D924, right on D112
Windmill
Open: Sunday afternoon mid-March to mid-November. Groups

by previous arrangement, Monday to Saturday, mid-March to mid-November.
☎ 54 81 31 35

Mennetou-sur-Cher
Thirteenth-century church. Apply to Town Hall.

Meusnes
Musée de la Pierre à fusil
Mairie, 7km (5 miles) south-west of Selles-sur-Cher, on D956 and D17
Flint knapping museum
Open: mornings only, Tuesday to Saturday, all year.
☎ 54 71 00 23

Montoire-sur-le-Loir
Chapelle St Gilles
Open: daily all year. Twelfth-century murals.

Neuvy-sur-Beuvron
Apply to house facing church to see fifteenth-century statues and seventeenth-century painting.

Oisly
'La Presle', Souvenirs de l'Agriculture et de la Viticulture anciennes
3km (2 miles) south of Contres on D675, right on D21 for 3km (2 miles)
Museum of traditional agricultural and viticultural techniques.
Open: Tuesday and Saturday afternoon, mid-June to mid-September.
☎ 54 79 52 69

Pontlevoy
Ancienne abbaye
Guided visits (45 mins) daily, July to mid-September; April to June daily but closed on Monday.

Romorantin-Lanthenay

Musée de Sologne
Hôtel de Ville, Faubourg St Roch
Museum of local ethnology.
Open: daily except Tuesday and
Sunday all year.
☎ 54 76 07 06 ext 423

*Musée Municipal de la Course
Automobile*
29-32 Faubourg d'Orléans
Racing car museum.
Open: daily all year except
Tuesday and Sunday morning.
☎ 54 76 07 06 ext 429

*Musée Archéologique M. de
Marcheville*
Le Carroir Doré, La Chancellerie,
14 Rue de la Résistance
Private archaeological collection.
Open: daily all year by previous
arrangement.
☎ 54 76 22 06

St Laurent-Nouan

Centrale Nucléaire St Laurent A & B
Nuclear power station
Observation platform, small
exhibition room and information
centre open daily all year. Visit to
power station.
Tour in English, (150 mins) by
previous arrangement (2 months'
notice in writing), Monday to
Saturday all year.
☎ 54 78 52 52

Selles-sur-Cher

*Musée municipal d'Histoire et de
Traditions Locales*
Cloître de l'Ancienne Abbaye
Museum of local history and
traditions.
Open: Saturday and Sunday, and
Tuesday and Thursday morning,

July and August. At other times by
previous arrangement.
☎ 54 97 40 10

Talcy

Moulin à vent
Windmill
Open: Sunday afternoon only, May
to mid-October.
☎ 54 81 20 45

Thésée-la-Romaine

Musée Archéologique
Le Vaulx-St Georges
Museum of local Roman excava-
tions.
Open: each afternoon except
Tuesday, July and August.
☎ 54 71 40 20

Troo

Grotte Pétrifiante
Stalactites and petrified objects in
cave.
Parking nearby.
Open: daily, April to September.

Vendôme

Tour of old quarters from Office de
Tourisme, Rue Poterie
Tuesday to Saturday all year (30
mins). Commentaries and pamphlets in English.
☎ 54 77 05 07

Musée Municipal
Cloître de la Trinité
Religious art of Vendômois, period
furniture, faïence chinaware,
musical instruments, prehistory,
tools of ancient regional trades.
Open: daily all year except
Tuesday.
☎ 54 77 05 07

LOIRET

Beaugency

Tour of old quarters from Château
Dunois
Groups by previous arrangement
daily all year. Individuals on
Thursday afternoons.
☎ 38 44 53 64

Hôtel de Ville
Collection of embroideries and
Gobelin tapestries.
Open: daily all year except
Wednesday.
☎ 38 44 51 42

Aquarium
2 Promenade de Barchelin
Exotic fish.
Open: daily July to August, and
daily except Tuesday January to
June and September to December.
☎ 38 44 81 69

La Chapelle-St Mesmin

Grotte 'du Dragon'
Western outskirts of Orléans on
N152
Restored grotto of St Mesmin
underneath chapel.
Open: daily all year by previous
arrangement.
☎ 38 72 60 03

Châteauneuf-sur-Loire

*Musée de la Marine de Loire et du
Vieux Châteauneuf*
History of navigation on Loire.
Open: daily July to August; Sunday
afternoon rest of year.

Chécy

Musée de la Tonnellerie
1 Avenue de Patay, 10km (6 miles)
east of Orléans, off N60
Cooperage museum. Pamphlets in

English.
Open: Sunday afternoon, July to
September; daily in June by
previous arrangement.
☎ 38 62 72 45

Cléry-St André

15km (9 miles) south-west of
Orléans on D951, Basilique
(basilica) open daily all year. To
visit vault and oratory of Louis XI,
and Chapelle St Jacques, apply to
sacristan or presbytery, 1 Rue du
Cloître.
☎ 38 45 70 05

Dampierre-en-Burly

Centrale Nucléaire
13km (8 miles) north-west of Gien
on D952
Information centre of nuclear
power station open weekdays and
Saturday, Sunday and public
holidays afternoons. Guided visits
last about 3 hours including 75
mins of films.
☎ 38 29 70 04

Germigny-des-Prés

Carolingian Oratory
4.5km (3 miles) south-east of
Châteauneuf-sur-Loire on D60
Open: daily all year. Commentaries
in English available. Pamphlets in
English. Parking outside.
☎ 38 58 27 97

Gien

*Musée et Salle d'Exposition de la
Faïencerie*
Place de la Victoire, on D952 in
north-west suburb of Gien
Open: all year. Displays of old
pieces of Gien pottery in museum;
pottery in current production in
Salle d'Exposition. No children

under 12 years. Information, and appointments for factory visits.
☎ 38 67 00 05

Jargeau
Musée 'Le Médailleur Oscar Roty et son temps'
3 Place du Petit Cloître
Collection of sculpture, medals, coins in home of engraver Roty.
Open: Saturday afternoon and all day Sunday, June to September.
☎ 38 59 82 78

Meung-sur-Loire
Musée Gaston Couté
Mairie
Souvenirs of Montmarte songwriter. Museum being reorganised at time of writing.
☎ 38 44 42 88

Orléans
Tour of old quarters from Maison de Tourisme, Place Albert I
Taped English guide (150 mins) available all year. At other times of year groups by previous arrangement.
☎ 38 53 05 95

Musée Historique et Archéologique de l'Orléanais
Hôtel Cabu, Place Abbé Desnoyers
Prehistory and antiquity.
Open: daily all year except Tuesday and public holidays.
☎ 38 53 39 22

Maison Jeanne d'Arc
Place du Général de Gaulle
Exhibits relating to Joan of Arc.
Open: afternoon only, Tuesday to Sunday, January to April and November to December; daily except Monday, May to October.
☎ 38 42 25 45

Hôtel Toutin
Inner courtyard of sixteenth-century mansion
Open: at any time except Sunday, Monday and month of August.

Musée des Sciences Naturelles
2 Rue Marcel Proust
Natural history museum
Open: all day Wednesday and Sunday and afternoons only Monday, Tuesday, Thursday, Friday all year.
☎ 38 42 25 58

Musée des Beaux-Arts
1, rue F. Rabier
Open: daily all year except Tuesday.
☎ 38 53 39 22

Cathedral of Ste Croix
Open: daily all year. Guided visits of choir, crypt and treasury between 2 and 6pm in season. Pamphlets in English.
☎ 38 53 47 23

Collégiale St Aignan
Also crypt of St Avit.
Open: all year to groups by previous arrangement. Commentaries in English.
☎ 38 66 24 10

St Benoît-sur-Loire
Abbaye de Fleury
Open: daily all year except Saturday morning and all Sunday, outside times of services. Guided visits daily except Saturday morning and Sunday, May to September. Commentaries and pamphlets in English. Gregorian chant sung at Mass and Vespers on certain public holidays at 10.45am, and on weekdays at 11.45am.

Tigy

Musée de l'Artisanat Rural Ancien
60 Rue de Sally, 8km (5 miles)
south of Châteauneuf-sur-Loire on
D11
Museum of ancient crafts. Commentaries in English.
Open: Sunday afternoon, late April
to mid-October; daily for rest of
year to groups by previous
arrangement.
☎ 38 58 00 42

Vienne-en-Val

Salles d'Exposition Archéologique
Route de Tigy, 7.5km (5 miles)
south of Jargeau on D12
Archaeological museum open
Sunday afternoon, April to
November.
☎ 38 58 81 64

MAINE-ET-LOIRE

Angers

Single ticket gives access to the
four buildings below marked * as
well as to the Château (see under
Châteaux Open to the Public.

* Musée Jean Lurçat
4 Boulevard Arago
Tapestries by Jean Lurçat and
medieval hospital ward and
dispensary.
Open: daily all year except
Monday and public holidays.
☎ 41 87 41 06

* Musée des Beaux-Arts
Logis Barrault, Rue du Musée
Noted for complete collection of
plaster casts by sculptor David
d'Angers, as well as paintings of
nineteenth-century French school.
Open: daily except Monday and
public holidays.
☎ 41 87 41 06 for information.

* Cathedral Treasury
Open: daily except Sunday and
Monday, April to June; daily July
to September; all day for rest of
year from Tuesday to Saturday.
Closed on public holidays.
☎ 41 87 41 06 for information.

* Musée Turpin de Crissé
Hôtel Pincé, Rue Lenepveu
Japanese and Chinese ceramics;
Egyptian collection; Greek and
Etruscan vases.
Open: daily except Monday and
public holidays.
☎ 41 87 41 06 for information.

Préfecture
To visit seventeenth-century
buildings and Romanesque
cloisters, apply to porter.

Baugé

Hôpital St Joseph
Seventeenth-century hospital and
dispensary.
Open: daily. To view building,
enquire at reception office.

Chapelle des Filles du Coeur de Marie
Contains Croix d'Anjou
Open: all weekdays and Sunday
afternoon.
Ring doorbell of Community,
8 Rue de la Girouardière.

Beaulieu-sur-Layon

Caveau du Vin
Exhibition of old Anjou wine
bottles and glasses.
Open: daily all year.

La Boissière Abbey

10km (6 miles) south of Le Lude on
D307. Open: daily early August to
early September, late December to
January.

La Bourgonnière Chapel

6km (4 miles) west of St Florent-le-Viel on D751
Open: daily all year.

Dénezé-sous-Doué

Cavernes sculptés
5.5km (3¹/₂ miles) north of Doué-la-Fontaine on D69
Hundreds of grotesque and erotic carvings on walls of cave, dating from sixteenth century.
Open: daily all year from Easter to September.
☎ 41 59 15 40

Doué-la-Fontaine

Quartier des Douces, Arènes
Guided visits (30 mins) of quarries whose arena-like seats were carved in fifteenth century. Now used for concerts, plays and flower shows.
Open: all year except Tuesday out of season.
☎ 41 59 22 28

Fontevraud-l'Abbaye

Guided visits daily all year except Tuesday and public holidays, of church, cloisters, refectory and huge Romanesque kitchens. Abbey houses *Centre Culturel de Rencontre* of *Centre Culturel de l'Ouest*, where concerts, exhibitions and conferences are held.
☎ 41 51 71 41

Jarzé

Chapelle Notre Dame-de-Montplacé
2km (1 mile) north-east of Jarzé on D82, then right
Key to solitary and simple chapel at Maison des Religieuses, near Jarzé Church.

Linières-Bouton

South on D767 from Noyant for 7km (5 miles) right, and right again for village.
To see Plantagenet choir and seventeenth-century painting of Annunciation in church, ask for key at grocer's shop, Place de l'Eglise.

Liré

Musée Joachim du Bellay
Small museum of mementoes of sixteenth-century Angevin poet.
Open: daily except Monday.

Louresse-Rochemenier

Musée Paysan
6.5km (4 miles) north-west of Doué-la-Fontaine on D761
Peasant museum of old farm implements, costumes in cave, illustrating how peasants used to cultivate crops underground (45 mins).
Open: daily except Monday, April to October; in July and August also open Monday; open afternoons Saturday, Sunday and public holidays rest of year except December and January.
☎ 41 59 18 15

Montreuil-Bellay

Ancienne Abbaye d'Asnières
5.5km (3¹/₂ miles) on D761 towards Doué-la-Fontaine, right at Brossay for 2km (1 mile)
Guided visits (30 mins) of ruins of twelfth-century abbey and choir in Gothic Angevin style, daily July and August.

St Aubin-de-Luigné

Château de la Haute-Guerche
4km (2¹/₂ miles) south of
Rochefort-sur-Loire on D54, 1km
(¹/₂ mile) west on D125
Ruined fortress with wide views.
Open: daily July and August.

Saumur

Musée d'Arts Décoratifs and Musée du Cheval
Museum of Decorative Arts
contains varied collection of
medieval and Renaissance
decorative works; Horse Museum
presents history of riding.
Both located in Château; see
Châteaux Open to the Public
section for details.
☎ 41 51 03 06

Musée de la Cavalerie
Avenue Maréchal Foch
Guided visits (by appointment)
daily all year except August.

Musée des Blindés
Armoured vehicle museum
Open: daily all year.
☎ 41 51 05 43 ext 446

Ecole Nationale d'Equitation
St Hilaire-St Florent, western
suburb on south bank of Loire on
D751
Guided visits round National
Riding School arranged at Office de
Tourisme, 25 Place de la Bilange.
☎ 41 51 03 06

Musée du Champignon
St Hilaire-St Florent
Guided visits daily mid-March to
mid-November round cliff caves
where techniques of growing
different varieties of mushroom are
shown.
☎ 41 50 31 55

Dolmen de Bagneux
2km (1 mile) south on N147, left by
church on D160
Apply to Café-Restaurant du
Dolmen (drinks obligatory) for
entrance to enclosure to see one of
France's largest megalithic
monuments.

St Laurent-de-la-Plaine

Musée des Vieux Métiers
5km (3 miles) south-west of
Chalonnes on D762
Craftsmen's tools and techniques
used locally before industrial age.
Enquire locally for opening times.

Turquant

Musée de l'Outil
Moulin de la Herpinière (south of
Turquant), 8km (5 miles) east of
Saumur on south bank of Loire on
D947
Restored fifteenth-century mill
where statuary, paintings,
tapestries and hand-painted
wallpapers are made.
Open: daily all year, except
January.
☎ 41 51 75 22

SARTHE

Beaumont-Pied-de-Boeuf

Costume Museum
8km (5 miles) north of Château-du-
Loir on D73A
Open: daily mid-July to end
August and Sunday afternoon May
to September.
☎ 43 44 29 83

La Flèche

Prytanée National Militaire
One-time Jesuit college, now
preparatory school for military
colleges.

Open: daily (appointment necessary) during summer holidays.

Chapelle Notre Dame des Vertus
Open: daily. Apply to Maison d'Enfants next door to see over Romanesque building with Renaissance wood-carvings.

Jupilles
North on D73A from Château-du-Loir to Beaumont-Pied-de-Boeuf, right on D73, 12.5km (8 miles) Exhibition of traditional woodcraft (in heart of Forêt de Bercé, 13,750 acres).
Open: afternoons daily except Monday, mid-April to September.

Poncé-sur-le-Loir
Musée d'Ethnographie du Maine
Regional ethnographic museum in château.
Open: March to mid-November, daily except Sunday morning.

Atelier de la Volonnière
Exhibition and sale of work: leather, painted silks, antiques, dolls and painted furniture.
Open: daily all year, afternoon only on Sunday and public holidays.

Artisanant, Grès du Loir
Moulin de Paillard
Craft centre: pottery workshops, wrought-ironwork, woodwork, weaving, glass-blowing, lampshade making and wicker work. Exhibition and sales.
Open: daily all year, afternoon only on Sunday and public holidays.

Pringé
North-east on N23 from La Flèche for 5.5km ($3^1/_2$ miles) right at Clermont-Créans on D13 for 6km (4 miles)

Fifteenth-century church with sixteenth-century murals. Ask for key at last house on right at north exit of village.

Solesmes
Abbaye St Pierre
3km (2 miles) outside Sablé-sur-Sarthe
Only Abbey church open to public Famous Gregorian chant sung at Mass at 10am Sunday and 9.45am weekdays; Vespers at 5pm.
☎ 43 95 03 08

Annual Events

Amboise
Easter and 15 August — Wine Fair.

Angers
End of June to mid-July, Anjou festival of concerts, plays, ballet, exhibitions. (Many similar events are held at this time throughout Maine-et-Loire.)

Beaugency
June, drama festival at château.

Blois
Mid-June, *Floréal Blésois*, carnival, regatta, drama and music.

Bourges
May, *'La Vieille Ville en Fête'*, carnival.
May to October, audio-visual show, *'La Cathédrale de Bourges et les Monuments du Cher'*.

Bourgueil
First Saturday in February, Wine Fair.

Châteauneuf-sur-Loire
Whit Sunday, Rhododendron Festival.

Chênehutte
Around 1 May, Mushroom Fair.

Cheverny
Mid-July to mid-August, torchlight meet of hounds, and horn concerts by Trompes de Cheverny.

Chinon
First weekend in August, medieval market held in period costume, tasting of old recipes, medieval trades, juggling, dancing and singing.

Cunault
Six Sundays a year between April and September, *Les Dimanches animées de Cunault*, market in village square featuring crafts and local produce, circus, street bands, folk groups, jugglers and refreshments.

Doué-la-Fontaine
Mid-July, *Floralies de la Rose*, International Rose Festival held in Arène (old quarry with stepped seats).

Gien
Mid-August, every other (odd) year. Historical Festival, drama shows and parades.

Jargeau
Mid-October, *Foire aux Chats* (or *châtaignes*), Chestnut Fair.

Langeais
Late July to early August, International Music Festivals at Domaine de Vernou.

Loches
Mid-July, peasant market.

Menetou-Salon
Mid-May, *Frairie des Brangers*, festival reconstructing past of village.

La Ménitré
Third Sunday in July. Local folklore groups, displays of ancient costumes and head-dresses.
24 December, *Messe des Naulets* in church.
Local folklore groups sing Christmas carols in patois, dressed in old regional costume.

Meung-sur-Loire
June and September, organ concerts at Collégiale St Liphard.

Molineuf
August, Bric-à-brac Fair.

Montoire-sur-le-Loir
Mid-August, World Folklore Festival each evening, street processions, concerts.

Olivet
Second week in June, watersports festival on River Loiret.

Orléans
7 and 8 May, Joan of Arc Festival. Illumination of cathedral on 7 May; religious and secular ceremonies on 8 May.
☎ 38 42 22 22
May to October, open-air floral displays in Parc Floral de la Source.
☎ 38 63 33 17

Sablé-sur-Sarthe
Last Sunday in May, *Fête du Quéniau* (Children's Festival), costumes, dancing.

St Benoît
Easter Saturday, Vigil and Easter ceremony, and Gregorian chant at abbey.
Christmas Eve, Gregorian chant at abbey.

Ste Maure-de-Touraine
June, Gastronomic Fair.

Saumur
Second fortnight in July, *Grand Carrousel*, cavalry display by Cadre Noir and military tattoo.
Mid-September, equestrian fortnight.

Solesmes
Holy Week, mass in abbey and Gregorian chant.
Christmas Eve, Midnight Mass.

Sully-sur-Loire
Whitsun week, orchestral concerts at château.
Friday and Saturday evenings in July, Music and drama festival at château.
Last Sunday in October, meet of hounds and concert of hunting horns at château.
☎ 38 53 05 95

Tours
Last weekend in June, first weekend in July, Music Festival of Touraine at Grange de Meslay, with international celebrities.
☎ 47 21 65 08.
May, international choral singing and flower pageant.
Last fortnight in July, Drama Festival.
Early August, Ballet Festival in garden of Musée des Beaux-Arts.

Rivers and Lakes

Many of the rivers and lakes are ready-made for watersports, bathing or just sunbathing on natural sandy or shingly river- and lake-side beaches. Others have been made into well-equipped centres for sailing, waterskiing,

windsurfing or fishing. A number of towns and villages have built swimming pools or sports complexes run by the municipality which are open to everyone.

Listed below are some of the lakes and riverside spots where there are beaches; all of them are safe. Elsewhere there can be a risk from deceptively strong currents, eddies or sand spits which look firm enough but may be water-logged quicksands.

Amboise (Loire), sailing; Ile d'Or leisure centre with swimming pool.
Angers (Maine), the Maine Lake, sailing, waterskiing.
Bléré (Cher), sailing.
Blois-les-Noëls, Lac du Loire (Loire), sailing, waterskiing and other leisure facilities.
Cerdon, Etang du Puits, extensive boating facilities.
Château-la-Vallière, Etang du Val Joyeux.
Châteauneuf-sur-Loire (Loire).
Chinon (Vienne), sailing, canoeing, fishing.
Coëmont (Loir).
Combreux, Etang de la Vallée, all watersports, hire of boats and pedaloes.
Gien (Loire).
Le Gué-du-Loir (Loir).
Ingrandes (Loire).
Langeais (Loire), sailing.
Loches (Indre), nautical centre with open-air and covered and heated swimming-pools.
Marcon, Lac des Varennes, canoeing, fishing, sailing, windsurfing.
Montsoreau (Loire), sailing, waterskiing.
Noven-sur-Sarthe (Sarthe).
Orléans (Loire), beaches of Ile

Arrault and Ile Charlemagne.
Orléans (Loiret), canoeing.
Parcé-sur-Sarthe (Sarthe).
Les Ponts-de-Cé (Loire).
Rille, Lac de Pincemaille.
Saumur (Loire), sailing,
waterskiing.
Le Thoureil (Loire), sailing,
waterskiing.
Tours (Loire), sailing, canoeing.
Tours (Cher), lake and park of St
Avertin, sailing, pedaloes,
swimming-pool, fishing.
Vaas (Loir).

Boating Holidays and River Cruises

Hiring a boat or taking a river
cruise offers the chance to gain a
quite different perspective on this
part of France. A selection of ideas
are shown below.

Angers
Boat and barge excursions along
River Layon. Cruises along Rivers
Sarthe, Mayenne and Loire with
lunch on board. Cruiser hire (for
day, weekend, week or longer) for
whole Bassin de la Maine. There
are 250km (155 miles) of water-
ways along Sarthe (twenty locks
between Angers and Le Mans),
Mayenne (twenty-five locks
between Angers and Laval),
Oudon (three locks between Segré
and Le Lion d'Angers). Excursions
can include bicycle and tent hire
and opportunities for white fish
angling. Boat-hire companies offer
boats of various types, based at
Angers and other centres.
  Information and booking for all
centres through Maine Reservation,

Maison du Tourisme, Place
Kennedy, 49000 Angers.
☎ 41 88 23 85

Beaugency
Kayak and cycling holidays for 2
weeks for people between ages of
18 and 30 who are swimmers.
Overnight accommodation in
Youth Hostels and tents on certain
dates in July and August. First
week cycling: Beaugency to
Châtillon-sur-Loire. Second week
kayaking: Châtillon to Beaugency.
  Information from Loisirs-
Accueil-Loiret, 3 Rue de la
Bretonnerie, 45000 Orléans.
☎ 38 62 04 88

Briare
Cruises on board traditional *peniche*
along the Canal de Briare ($1^1/_2$hrs
and 3hrs); also cruiser hire.
  Information from: Loisirs
Accueil, 3 rue de la Bretonnerie,
45000 Orléans.
☎ 38 62 04 88

Chaumont
Cruises on the Loire, daily from
July to mid-September (90 mins)

Châteauneuf-sur-Sarthe
Boat-hire centre on River Sarthe.
Cruises on Roi René I or Roi René
II, 15 June to 15 September.

Chenillé-Changé
Boat-hire centre on River Mayenne.

Grez-Neuville
Boat-hire centre on River Mayenne.

Malicorne-sur-Sarthe
Boat-hire centre.

Noyen-sur-Sarthe
Boat-hire centre.

Orléans
Cruises on the River Loiret, also lunchtime cruise which includes meal.

Sablé-sur-Sarthe
Boat-hire centre. Also cruises of 110 mins by the *Sablésien* (85 passengers) with commentary along River Sarthe; Friday and Saturday at 4.45pm between end June and mid-August.

Cruisers can also be hired through Hoseasons Holidays, Sunway House, Lowestoft, Suffolk, NR32 3LT, ☎ 0502 500 505; or Blakes Holidays, Wroxham, Norfolk. ☎ 0603 784131

Fishing

Fast-running tributaries of the Loire (like the Loire itself well-upstream in its more mountainous course) are rated First Category with trout predominating. Open season runs from the third Saturday in February to the last Monday in September.

In the Loire Valley region, the Loire and slow-running tributaries are Second Category, with coarse fish forming the majority. Open season is from mid-June to mid-April.

At many places fishing is authorised. Permits issued by the *département* are for a whole year. Shops selling fishing tackle are sometimes able to issue permits for a fee. At some privately owned lakes, day permits are provided

against payment.

Fish likely to be found in the rivers include; bream, bullhead, carp, grey mullet, perch, pike, roach, shad, trout and zander.

Walking

There are plenty of footpaths for those who want to take short walks. Long-distance walks along marked paths (Sentiers de Grande Randonnée) are shown by broken lines on Michelin maps which also give route numbers, eg GR3 or GR46. A number of these pass through the Loire Valley. You can follow the north bank of the Loire from Orléans to Blois. Others criss-cross Sologne (one route goes from Gien to Chambord), the Indre Valley and Vendômois. They also pass through Orléans Forest, the largest in France.

Most local tourist offices can supply information and sketch maps of interesting paths in the vicinity. For much more detailed guidance, it is wise to join the nationwide organisation, Comité National des Sentiers de Grande Randonnée, 92 Rue de Clignancourt, 75883 Paris. ☎ 1 259 60 40. Ask at tourist offices for information about nature trails or guides who give instruction about local flora and fauna.

The main long distance paths in the Loire Valley are:
GR3 — The Loire Valley 275km (170 miles)
GR41 — The Cher Valley 51km (32 miles)
GR46 — The Indre Valley 125km (78 miles)

GR48 — The Valleys of the Vienne, Creuse, and Gartempe 203km (126 miles)

Wildlife, Zoos and Gardens

Angers
Arboretum de la Maulévrie
Jardin des Plantes
off Boulevard Carnot.
Exotic trees.

Forêt de Bercé
Guided visits round Futaie des Clos by official of National Forestry Office, daily except Tuesday, at 9.30am and 3pm. Point of departure: Chêne Boppe parking area east of Jupilles.

Châteauneuf-sur-Loire
Arboretum du Château
Mostly giant rhododendrons in grounds of château.
Open: daily all year.
☎ 38 58 41 18

Doué-la-Fontaine
Zoo des Minières
300 animals in disused quarries.
Open: all year.

La Flèche
Parc Zoologique du Tertre Rouge
5km (3 miles) south-east on D104.
Open: all day all year. Wide variety of wild animals in 18 acres of forest; small natural history museum with dioramas of regional fauna.
☎ 43 94 04 55

Le Lion-d'Angers
Haras National (National Stud)
Château Isle-Briand
Open: all year (appointment necessary). Visit to saddle-room, smithy, riding-school and stables of different breeds of horses including retired race-horses at stud.
Displays of harnesses and stallions between October and February at 2.30pm on first Wednesday of each month.

La Ferté-St Aubin
Domaine Solognot du Ciran
6km (4 miles) east of town, left at Les Quatre
Routes on D108, left after 1km ($^1/_2$ mile)
Sologne wildlife and walks through characteristic Sologne countryside (1-2 hours; boots advisable).
Open: daily all year. Advance notice required for groups, and those wanting guided tours. Small museum of Sologne bygones in château.
☎ 38 76 52 72

Orléans-la-Source
Parc Floral at Olivet
Open: afternoons, January to March and mid-November to December. Daily April to mid-November. Pamphlets in English. Floral park and animals; greenhouse-restaurant. Miniature train (25 mins) in Floral Park runs afternoons only on Wednesday, Friday and Saturday, April; afternoons daily except Thursday, May to September; afternoons only, Wednesday, Friday and Saturday, October.
☎ 38 63 33 17

Richelieu
Gardens of château
Open: daily all year. 45 hectares of
formal grounds belonging to
University of Paris.

St Aignan-sur-Cher
Parc Ornithologique de Beauval
4km (2¹/₂ miles) south of St Aignan
on D675. Bird sanctuary concen-
trating on endangered species.
Open: all year daily until nightfall.
☎ 54 75 05 56

St Denis-de-l'Hôtel
Parc Floral Henri Coulland
Flower gardens.
Open: daily all year.

Valençay
Zoo et Parc du Château
Zoo in grounds of château.
Open: daily mid-March to mid-
September only Saturday and
Sunday, January to mid-March.
☎ 54 00 10 66

Verneuil-sur-Indre
Floral gardens run by horticultural
college in grounds of château.
Open: between June and October.

Villandry
Jardin du Château
Formal gardens.
Open: daily all year.
☎ 47 50 02 09

Steam Railways

Marcilly-sur-Maulne
West of Château-la-Vallière, *Train à
vapeur*
Narrow-gauge railway, 2km (1
mile) track, and collection of
engines, etc.

Open: Sunday afternoon, July and
August for trip with old steam
locomotive (or sometimes diesel)
on certain dates. Train available to
groups by previous arrangement,
Monday to Saturday.
☎ 47 24 07 95

Chinon-Richelieu-Chinon
Trains à vapeur de Touraine
Steam train journeys, single or
return, on Sunday from early May
to mid-September, using early
twentieth-century rolling-stock.
Leisurely trip through fields,
vineyards and woodlands with
wayside halts for local wine- and
cheese-tasting. Information at
Chinon railway station, SNCF
☎ 47 58 12 97

**Salbris—Buzançais; Romorantin-
Lanthenay — Salbris —
Romorantin-Lanthenay**
(Loir-et-Cher and Indre)
Special steam train excursions.
Details from Salbris Syndicat
d'Initiative
☎ 54 83 06 54.

From the Air

Short trips by light aircraft are
available from the following
airfields; one or two also use
helicopters.

Tours Aéro Services
Tours-Sorigny
37250 Montbazon
Circuit of châteaux.
☎ 47 51 25 68

Les Ailes Tourangelles
Aerodrome d'Amboise-Dierre
☎ 47 57 93 91

Aero-Club de Sologne
4 Rue des Trois-Rois
41200 Romorantin-Lanthenay

Aérodrome du Breuil
Villefrancoeur
41000 Blois
☎ 54 78 55 50 (Loisirs-Accueil)

Aérodrome Orléans-Saran
Choice of three 20 minute circuits;
aircraft carry five passengers.
☎ 38 62 04 88 (Loisirs-Accueil)

Air Adventure
Hot-air balloon flights in fine
weather.
☎ 80 26 63 30

Wine-tasting

In all wine-producing areas there
are *caves* (cellars) which offer
dégustation (tasting). They range
from large co-operatives selling
local table wine to small private
caves which are outlets for the
produce of a single vineyard. Wine
can be bought in single bottles or in
bulk. Most places do not charge for
entrance and you can usually go in
unannounced during the opening
times of the establishment. A few
are visited by previous arrangement only.

Cher
Menetou-Salon
Caves Gilbert
Les Faucards.
☎ 48 64 80 77

Preuilly
Cave de l'Union Viticole
Le Carroir
☎ 48 51 30 78

Indre-et-Loire
Amboise
Cave Denay
La Briquetterie.
☎ 47 57 11 53

Amboise
Cave Girault-Artois
7 Quai des Violettes
☎ 47 57 07 71

Bourgueil
Cave Touristique de la Dive-
Bouteille
Chevrette
☎ 47 97 72 01

Chançay
Cave Vigneau-Chevreau
4 Rue de Clos Baguelin
☎ 47 52 93 22

Chinon
Musée du Vin
Rue du Dr Gendron

Chinon
Cave Plouzeau
rue Voltaire
☎ 47 93 16 34

Chinon
Cave Montplaisir
Quai Pasteur
☎ 47 93 20 75

Ligré
Cave Manzagol
La Noblaie
☎ 47 93 10 96

Limeray
Cave Dutertre
20-21 Rue d'Enfer
☎ 47 30 10 69

Montlouis-sur-Loire
Cave Coopérative des Producteurs
de Vins de Montlouis
2 Route de St Aignan
☎ 47 50 82 26

Tours
Maison des Vins de Touraine
Square Prosper Mérimée
☎ 47 05 40 01

Vouvray
Cave Coopérative des Producteurs
des Grands Vins de Vouvray
Vallée Coquette
☎ 47 52 75 03

Vouvray
Cave des Viticulteurs du Vouvray
route de Vernou
☎ 47 52 60 20

Vouvray
Cave Daniel Jarry
La Caillerie
Route de la Vallée Coquette
☎ 47 52 78 75

Vouvray
Cave de la Bonne Dame
Wine Fair early January and 15
August.

Loir-et-Cher
Cellettes
Cave Dorléans
Domaine de la Gaudronnière
☎ 54 44 20 41

Chémery
Cave de la Grande Brosse
☎ 54 71 81 03

Chissay-en-Touraine
Distillerie 'Fraise d'Or'
62 Route de Tours
Manufacture of strawberry liqueur.
☎ 54 32 32 05

Mesland
Caves Brosillon
Domaine de Lusqueneau
☎ 54 70 28 23

Montrichard
Caves Montmousseau

71 Rue de Vierzon
☎ 54 32 07 04

Seur
Cave A Coutoux
5 Chemin des Murs
☎ 54 44 04 58

Loiret
Beaulieu-sur-Loire
Cave de M. Guerot, 'L'Etang'.
☎ 38 35 81 58

Mareau-aux-Prés
Cave Coopérative
550 Route des Muids.
☎ 38 45 61 08

Olivet
Covifruit, 613 Rue du Pressoir-
Tonneau
☎ 38 63 40 20

Maine-et-Loire
Angers
Distillerie Cointreau
St Barthélémy d'Anjou
☎ 41 41 25 21

Angers
Maison du Vin
☎ 41 88 81 13

Angers
Distillerie Giffard
☎ 41 34 52 23

Liré
Cave Du Bellay
☎ 41 83 03 26

Louresse-Rochemenier
Cave et Musée
☎ 41 59 13 13

St Cyr-en-Bourg
Cave Coopérative des Vignerons
de Saumur
☎ 41 51 61 09

St Hilaire-St Florent
Caves Ackerman-Laurence
☎ 41 50 25 33

St Hilaire-St Florent
Caves Bouvet-Ladubay
☎ 41 50 11 12

St Hilaire-St Florent
Cave de Neuville
☎ 41 50 16 43

St Hilaire-St Florent
Cave Veuve Amiot
☎ 41 50 25 24

Saumur
Cave Gratien-Meyer
☎ 41 51 04 54

Saumur
Maison du Vin
☎ 41 51 16 40

Sarthe
Chahaignes
Cave M. Bouin
Société La Malvoyère
☎ 43 44 46 19

La Chartre-sur-le-Loir
Cave M. Gigou
☎ 43 44 48 72

La Chartre-sur-le-Loir
Cave M. Barbier
☎ 43 44 40 82

L'Homme
Cave M. Pinon
'Les Tuffières'
☎ 43 85 30 56

L'Homme
Cave M. Boutard
'La Varenne'
☎ 43 44 43 63

L'Homme
Cave M. Branjonneau
'Les Jasnières'
☎ 43 79 03 53

L'Homme
Cave M. Cartereau
'Bordebeurre'
☎ 43 44 48 66

Marçon
Cave M. Cronier
'Le Bourg'
☎ 43 44 13 20

Vouvray-sur-Loir
Cave Municipale
Mairie
☎ 43 44 14 15

INDEX

A Note to the Reader

We hope you have found this book informative, helpful and enjoyable. It is always our aim to make our publications as accurate and up to date as possible. With this in mind, we would appreciate any comments that you might have. If you come across any information to update this book or discover something new about the area we have covered, please let us know so that your notes may be incorporated in future editions.

As it is MPC's principal aim to keep our publications lively and responsive to change, any information that readers provide will be a valuable asset to us in maintaining the highest possible standards for our books.

Please write to:
Senior Editor
Moorland Publishing Co Ltd
Free Post
Ashbourne
Derbyshire
DE6 9BR